"Ms. Bolls tells, in plain English, the benefits of meditation for everyone, but points out added benefits for Aspies, as well as illuminating why so many of us are drawn to and are good at meditation. She refreshingly debunks a lot of the mysticism and mystique surrounding the act. Yet she is highly schooled and practiced in many forms of meditation and is an enthusiastic champion of it as an oasis of calm in a whirlwind life, whether that whirlwind comes from external or internal sources. I highly recommend this fun and practical manual."

—*Rudy Simone, author of* Aspergirls: Empowering Females with Asperger Syndrome

"A great starting point for anyone diagnosed with Asperger Syndrome, or professionals working with people with Asperger Syndrome, interested in meditation as a tool for relaxation. Bolls makes meditation practice widely accessible in a secular as well as spiritual context beyond myths and misconceptions."

—*Chris Mitchell, author of* Asperger's Syndrome and Mindfulness: Taking Refuge in the Buddha

"If I were asked to give one piece of advice to anybody coping with Asperger Syndrome, it would be to learn to meditate. Amidst the chaos that surrounds us, you may find increased security, calm, and self-control all at your command. Meditation saved my life when I was 20, a quarter century before I even knew I was an Aspie. Ulrike Domenika Bolls' wonderful book may comfort many more of us."

—*Tim Page, professor at the University of Southern California and author of* Parallel Play

D1270040

of related interest

Asperger Syndrome and Mindfulness
Taking Refuge in the Buddha
Chris Mitchell
ISBN 978 1 84310 686 9
eISBN 978 1 84642 888 3

Mind/Body Techniques for Asperger Syndrome
The Way of the Pathfinder
Ron Rubio
Forewords by Irene Brody and Anthony Castrogiovanni
ISBN 978 1 84310 875 7
eISBN 978 1 84642 805 0

The Complete Guide to Asperger Syndrome
Tony Attwood
ISBN 978 1 84310 495 7 (hardback)
ISBN 978 1 84310 669 2 (paperback)
eISBN 978 1 84642 559 2

Asperger Syndrome and Anxiety
A Guide to Successful Stress Management
Nick Dubin
Foreword by Valerie Gaus
ISBN 978 1 84310 895 5
eISBN 978 1 84642 922 4

A Self-Determined Future with Asperger Syndrome
Solution Focused Approaches
E. Veronica Bliss and Genevieve Edmonds
Foreword by Bill O'Connell, Director of Training, Focus on Solutions
ISBN 978 1 84310 513 8
eISBN 978 1 84642 685 8

Meditation for Aspies

Everyday Techniques to Help People with Asperger Syndrome Take Control and Improve their Lives

Ulrike Domenika Bolls

Translated by Rowan Sewell

Jessica Kingsley *Publishers*
London and Philadelphia

This edition published in 2013
by Jessica Kingsley Publishers
116 Pentonville Road
London N1 9JB, UK
and
400 Market Street, Suite 400
Philadelphia, PA 19106, USA

www.jkp.com

First published in German in 2012

Copyright © Ulrike Domenika Bolls 2012, 2013
Translation copyright © Rowan Sewell 2013

Library of Congress Cataloging in Publication Data
A CIP catalog record for this book is available from the Library of Congress

British Library Cataloguing in Publication Data
A CIP catalogue record for this book is available from the British Library

ISBN 978 1 84905 386 0
eISBN 978 0 85700 756 8

Printed and bound in Great Britain

Contents

Preface

My first steps in meditation

I first came into contact with meditation aged 20. At the time, I was receiving psychotherapy due to panic attacks and depression. The meditation exercises that my therapist showed me over the course of three years were primarily intended to calm me down during the acute phases of emotional meltdown which I would experience on an almost daily basis. The exercises were also aimed at helping me lead a more balanced life in the long term and deal with stress better. These reasons alone are already two excellent examples of why meditation is so helpful.

I had not been diagnosed with Asperger's then. In fact, I had been meditating since long before my diagnosis. With hindsight and the knowledge of my condition, I can now understand why I have spent so much time meditating in my life thus far. The two reasons stated above were the initial trigger; the desire to discover my inner self was another driving force which came later on.

But let us first proceed in chronological order. Aged 24, I lived near a yoga center and that motivated me to learn this discipline. I completed several yoga courses and an introductory course in meditation there. However, I didn't particularly enjoy the techniques I was taught at the center. In retrospect, I now realize that the atmosphere in the center was too stressful and rigid for my delicate senses. In one evening session, for example, I was forbidden from sitting with my legs stretched out in front of me and from touching my meditation chain with a certain finger because this finger was thought of as unclean in the culture practiced at the center. This was not my world.

Nevertheless, I had gained enough knowledge to practice yoga and meditation at home in my own private environment and at my own pace. Since then, both methods have accompanied me through the various phases of my life. At the time, I set up a type of "altar" for meditation at home, which was quite simply a small table with a candle placed on top of it. I would sit down in front of it, close my eyes and retreat to within myself. It allowed me to switch off and recharge my batteries. I have to admit, back then I wasn't as successful at doing this as I am today. But thankfully I wasn't able to make the comparison at the time. Given the pain I experienced in the previous years it was a vast improvement.

Over the course of the next ten years I stepped up my meditation. I learned a lot in meditation groups and diligently continued this practice at home. I was motivated by the thought of one day being able to sit down and simply switch off my thoughts. To bask in peace within my head. This thought alone seemed like paradise to me, so much so that I persisted intensively with learning many different types of meditation, and without planning it, the quest to find my inner self began to creep into my practice. I started thinking about who I really am. I wanted to find my place in the world, understand myself and others, most of whom were so often a puzzle to me. My own access to feelings of empathy and my sensory perception grew finer, my ability to deal with my emotions improved and the number of meltdowns reduced substantially.

Up to that point, my meditation practice had simply consisted of passive seated meditation. I was then introduced to forms of active meditation in meditation groups, such as

Dynamic Meditation, whirling and Nadabrahma meditation. This truly opened my eyes because I had the feeling that I was suddenly challenging my entire being, including my body.

I could feel that it was doing me good! I therefore set myself a hefty pace and never meditated for less than one hour a day—usually more. I had the feeling that by meditating I was doing something for myself, treating myself to something good, caring for myself and equipping myself to deal with the challenges of life. I slowly made progress and sensed I was becoming a calmer person in general. Over time, I learned to bring some order to my emotional chaos. Meditation, and therefore communication with my inner self, became a fixture in my daily routine.

I was so enthusiastic about it that I soon began working with other people, sharing my knowledge and experiences with them, sometimes in groups but largely on an individual basis. During this period, I took a great interest in esoteric topics and this also formed my source of income at the time. I felt at home in these groups, true to the Asperger's motto "wanting to belong but not wanting to belong at the same time," up to the point that I felt enough security in myself that I could continue on my path of professional and personal development alone.

Nowadays, I distance myself from esoteric thinking. However, in hindsight my esoteric years were very useful for me, not least because I learned to constructively question and independently assess the many concepts encompassed by esoteric and religious traditions. This gave me a new sense of freedom, inner security and authority. The challenge of being independent is something I strive to pass on to my clients in my work nowadays.

It required almost 15 years of constant work to reach the stage where I was not only able to experience a peaceful mind for a few moments, but was actually able to draw on it at will.

I knew who I was, and who I wasn't. And that was exactly what I had aimed to achieve.

Zazen (seated meditation following the Zen tradition) was the type of meditation which I last came into contact with and which I almost exclusively practice nowadays. However, I do not meditate within the framework of the rules and concepts practiced in Zen groups. Nevertheless, I stay true to the essence of Zazen—sitting in front of the white wall. Sitting within myself.

My life with Asperger's

You might be thinking that there wasn't much reference to Asperger's in the story so far! That's absolutely true, because up to this point, I had not even discovered this word to describe my characteristics.

I've always been interested in Autism and Asperger's, and was an avid reader of reports and biographies about them. I always had the feeling that so many aspects were reflected within me. However, I had not considered for one moment that I would fall within the diagnosis spectrum. I was getting on with life and I thought it was normal that life was so difficult. I knew that I was highly sensitive, and that I reacted much more sensitively to the things around me than most other people. I knew that I was intrapersonal and gifted spiritually. I define spirituality as the spiritual connection to transcendence completely independent of any religious and esoteric concepts. In spiritual terms, my gift was reflected by the fact that the process of self-discovery seemed to come much more easily to me than to other people around me.

I therefore got to know my characteristics, peculiarities, quirky habits and problems, but I only discovered that this had a special name when I was an adult. When I received the diagnosis, I therefore already knew my essence—who I am, what I am and how I am. At the same time, the diagnosis felt like a relief because it suddenly and conclusively explained *why* I am the way I am. And in relation to meditation, it also explained why I threw myself into meditation practice with such concentration and why it formed such a key source of support.

I decided that since the first half of my life had been such hard work, I would at least do my best to make the second half as easy as possible. I looked at what factors influence me and developed solutions to make life easier for myself in these areas. As I had already been working as a coach for over ten years, I was able to draw on a wealth of experience in tailoring solutions to fit personal circumstances.

I came to the basic realization that I'd already done a pretty good job in laying the foundations for a happy life. Only seemingly small details were left to be optimized. The main reason for my satisfaction in life was the knowledge of my inner self, which I have worked vigorously to develop since the age of 20. Meditation played a huge role in achieving this.

How I came to write this book

It was only at this point that I realized what a great asset meditation can be for people with Asperger Syndrome. We have a need for inner peace in a world full of stimuli, but also have the ability to passionately and single-mindedly pursue a topic.

Over the last few years, I have read a lot of books covering meditation. Some were good and others not so good, but only a few really got to the heart of the issue in my opinion. I felt that lots of these books talked too much theory instead of offering practical tips.

There are numerous meditation books available on the market, but none as yet specifically aimed at us Aspies. We tick differently. After asking around my friends and acquaintances with Asperger Syndrome, it was clear that there is definite demand for a book which focuses on meditation for Aspies.

The idea of writing this book then evolved inside me. I knew I was well qualified to do it: I have spent more than 10,000 hours of my life trying to get to know myself in courses, seminars, training and in my peaceful room. Nowadays, I work as a coach for highly gifted and sensitive people, including people with Asperger's. I offer help and training in meditation, and support people in finding their inner home, as indicated by my company name Highmat®, which is a play on the German word for "home." I can draw on personal and professional experience to offer deep insights into meditation, and over the years I've collected a wide range of tips, tricks, practices and easy steps to help others on their way.

I had to do it. I sat down and started to write. Now you have the end product in your hands. All the tips contained within this book as well as the descriptions and texts stem from the experiences which I gained through my own meditation and work with clients. This book can help you make a great start in a new chapter of your life, not through condescending instructions but through the tips of a good friend.

Now it's up to you, so let's go!

Introduction

I'm not going to lie, learning meditation in five minutes (as is often demanded and indeed promised in the modern age) is simply not possible. Learning meditation is a gradual, ongoing process. Deciding to meditate can change your life and as you are already holding this book in your hands, I assume that you are aiming to make a change. Perhaps you would like more inner peace, relaxation and balance. Perhaps you would like to gain some clarity about who you really are, as well as greater insight into your inner self. Perhaps your aim is closer contact with your emotions, allowing you to get to know them better and therefore to be in a position to deal with them better. All of these can be achieved through meditation.

Every Aspie has special characteristics which make his or her life and personality unique. Some more, some less. After all, everyone is their own very individual mix. Meditation is just as individual as the people who meditate. If you ask the question "What is meditation?" you will probably receive just as many different answers as the number of people you ask.

There is of course no specific meditation for Aspies. Or even for combating Asperger Syndrome. However, there are specific aspects of meditation which make the introduction to and practice of meditation easier for Aspies. In this book,

I highlight aspects of Asperger Syndrome from the point of view of meditation. How can our characteristics support us in our meditation? Which types of meditation are suitable for our characteristics? How can people with Asperger Syndrome particularly benefit from meditation? You will find the answers to these questions later in the book.

My book is aimed at newcomers to meditation. It includes preparations and exercises for everyday life, information about types of meditation, a checklist for practicing meditation and a broad practical overview of the topic of meditation in general. The scope offered by my open-minded approach can also give advanced learners a fresh insight into their meditation practice, allowing new freedom and inspiration.

My approach to meditation is free of religious and esoteric concepts. It is formulated in a neutral way and calls for an independent and responsible use of meditation which questions and redefines conventions. Although I've learned lots of different specific meditation traditions, I no longer practice them today. My concern is much more the essence of meditation, which is not connected to any rules, traditions or belief systems. The essence is what sets each meditation apart, when you are concentrating solely on yourself and coming into contact with your inner self. This is the basis for every form of meditation, irrespective of over-arching concepts.

People say that meditation is a lifelong process, Asperger Syndrome too. No wonder they suit each other so well. But beyond that, what many Aspies don't know is that Asperger's provides abilities which can actually help during meditation. In Chapter 5 "Welcoming Meditation into Your Everyday Life" and Chapter 9 "Top Tips..." you will find both general tips and suggestions specifically aimed at Aspies.

I will repeat certain concepts in different parts of the book, as I want to allow readers to select the chapters which primarily interest them. Throughout the book, you will also find cross references to other chapters, which is intended to make the book easier to use.

The language used in this book is also tailored to Aspies. Personally, I love language and enjoy playing with words. However, many Aspies find it difficult to understand complex idioms and imagery. I had the same problem in the past, but perhaps my love of playing with language helped me develop a lively turn of phrase. However, here I will use simple, clear language in an attempt to avoid any misunderstandings. At this point, I would also like to thank my translator Rowan, who is carefully transferring my style into English.

Let's get going so you can start meditating as soon as possible!

Chapter 1

What is Meditation?

Common misconceptions about meditation

As I've already been meditating for over half my life, I've certainly heard plenty of misconceptions voiced about meditation over the years. Here, I'd like to touch on the most common ones so you can get started without any negative feelings.

Misconception: "Meditation is only for do-gooders and wimps."

This view likely gained momentum in the 1970s and 1980s. At that time, meditation was mostly practiced by hippies or people with alternative lifestyles (which at the time was almost used as an insult) who came back from travels to India with crazy haircuts and new names.

However, this misconception still lives on today to a certain extent. Indeed, many people who you meet at meditation groups or centers may well fall into these categories. This can often stem from an exaggerated or desired (and sometimes just fake) representation of inner balance and a misunderstood sense of belonging. This can lead to normal human characteristics from the range of our feelings, such as anger, irritability or impatience being suppressed. As a result, these people may seem soft, quietly spoken and blissful. That is certainly not a state which you need to try to imitate or strive to attain.

A wish to "do good" can extend into the meditation itself. The intention of the meditation for these people might therefore be as follows: "I wish to have compassion and love for all people and beings in the universe." Although this is no doubt a noble cause, I believe that it is somewhat wide of the mark when it comes to the purpose of meditation.

Meditation is about you, not about everyone else and all the other beings in the universe. And if you want to concentrate on other people, in my view, the aim should not be loving all people and beings, but instead achieving a well-reflected and mature way of dealing with others. If you attend a meditation group which supports such a view, I recommend turning the sentence around for yourself: "I show compassion to myself and love myself." Applying this concept towards all people and beings starts with you. How can you love others if you don't love yourself? And let's face it, this task alone is hard enough.

As I see it, meditation is something for perfectly normal people who experience all the feelings and cravings that life has to offer.

Misconception: "Meditation is only for ascetics."

This misconception is comparable to the previous one and stems from similar ideas. It also evolves out of a form of exaggeration, artificial regulation and negation of your own needs. An example: "If I meditate, then I don't want to use any animal-related products and only drink fresh spring water. Since I started meditating for five hours a day, I now only need to sleep for five hours." Just like everything else, you can have too much of a good thing, and the same applies to meditation. Meditation time cannot come at the cost of your health. I'm a strong advocate of a balanced, healthy diet and sufficient sleep. In other words, you don't need to be an ascetic to meditate.

Misconception: "I need a group to meditate because the energy is much stronger in a group."

My answer to this is always: "If you need a group to meditate, you still have a lot of meditation to do!" If you believe in concepts like energy, then do not use them as an excuse not to meditate. Meditation is about inner communication with yourself. That is a monologue. For that you don't need anything or anyone you don't already have. You could call it a dialogue between yourself and your subconscious— between "me, myself and I," if you will.

This misconception usually stems from the fact that individuals who believe that they can meditate better in a group cannot independently motivate themselves to start meditating or maintain meditation—or cannot simply stand true contact themselves. In these cases, the group is a great source of help in overcoming your inner sloth but also a source of distraction. Meditation is therefore possible in a group, but a group is not essential.

Misconception: "I've meditated before but it didn't work. I don't think it's for me."

Many beginners take their first steps in meditation with excessively high expectations. They start with silent sitting meditation, which represents a major challenge for beginners, and they quickly become frustrated when they are unable to quiet their thoughts. One of my clients even once told me that he cut off his breathing for so long that he almost lost consciousness just so he could achieve a state of peace. I was shocked that such a dangerous approach was used to achieve something which stands in total contrast to what meditation is actually about, so please do not even think about giving this a try, not least because he was unsuccessful in achieving inner peace with this dangerous method. This story also attests to the desperation hidden inside, the unquenchable desire for peace.

And this is the first lesson in meditation: *patience*. Meditation is a long-term method which provides results gradually. Just like learning a musical instrument, a foreign language or a new sport, meditation requires practice and training before you experience first successes. You need to find the right methods which suit your way of learning, thinking and feeling. This book contains numerous tips to help beginners do just that.

Misconception: "Meditation is nothing but sitting around."

From the outside, passive meditation certainly might look that way, but as Aspies we know that people who seem peaceful on the outside can still be very active on the inside. And when you meditate, you are certainly active on the inside. When you start meditating, your mind is usually active and is constantly talking to you. The aim is to quiet your mind in an effort to achieve active peace.

As you will read in this book, there are also many types of active meditation which stand in stark contrast to passive, silent meditation, where you do not sit down but hop around, wriggle, dance and generally let off steam. In short, meditation is exercise for body and mind.

In the end, it doesn't matter if you are moving or sitting peacefully. Only you have the ability to make an activity into a meditation through your concentration, attitude and intentions. When you take on this challenge, sitting around quickly becomes meditation.

Misconception: "Meditation is boring."

This opinion relates to the fact that the conventional image of meditation is a person sitting still with eyes closed in peaceful harmony. It has to be said that this doesn't look like a particularly action-packed activity!

In a biographical film about Stephen Hawking (*A Brief History of Time*, 1991), his wife told a story about a party which they both attended. Stephen, an ALS (amyotrophic lateral sclerosis) sufferer, was sitting in his wheelchair quiet and alone in the corner. Then his wife went up to him and said: "Stephen, why don't you mingle with the guests a little? I know that you're perfectly happy, but the other people don't know that you're sitting there and having fun on your own." He was far from bored because he could think. He didn't need any amusement from the outside. His mind was enough. Whether Stephen Hawking had to put a lot of effort into setting his thoughts free or whether he had to overcome challenges, I wouldn't like to say. But this story offers a great comparison with the art of meditation. Although it looks boring from the outside, the process inside is what counts. And if you are honest with yourself, I guarantee you will never be bored with your mind and your thoughts.

Misconception: "You must be religious or spiritual to practice meditation."

Historically many meditative techniques derive from religious and spiritual practices—and not only from Eastern cultures as we often think, but from Christian traditions too. In our minds meditation is often associated with gods or Buddha. In esoteric traditions, no specific god is integrated into meditations but in its place there is a godly energy, angels or spirits. People also talk about energy, which flows through the body or stops flowing and can be released if you are blocked.

Although I am not religious, I grew up in a Christian household and on my journey of finding myself and my way into meditation, I came across many other different religions and beliefs. Because mediation has been so intrinsically connected to religion in the past, it may appear logical that meditation should be compulsorily connected to religions and many people have the impression that you can only meditate successfully when you believe in a form of religion.

But that is not the case, you do not need a connection to religion or spirituality to meditate. Meditation is open to all beliefs, be they religious or of an atheist nature. If religion is part of your life it can be a valuable part of your meditation. If, on the other hand, religious or spiritual beliefs are not a part of your life you will still be able to meditate successfully. It is my view that without concepts like this you are ultimately able to concentrate completely on yourself to an even greater extent.

Different religions come with different rules when it comes to meditation. But those are an extraneous garment to the meditation practice. You are not required to place a Buddha figure on your meditation altar in order to experience good meditation. You don't have to ask for the power of the angels to have an intense meditation experience. You don't have to sit perfectly straight to allow the energy for a meditation to flow. Meditation is about you. If belief is part of you, then it is also part of your meditation. If belief does not play any role in your life, then it should not be artificially integrated into your meditation.

Misconception: "I'm too old to learn to meditate."

This statement is a common misconception and an excuse in equal measure. One thing is certain: no one is too old to learn how to meditate. Even if I write a number of times that it will probably take many years until your mind has finally reached peace, tangible results and an improvement in quality of life can generally be seen after only a few months. This makes the argument that you never see the results of your effort slightly unconvincing.

Another fact is also clear: you will have Asperger Syndrome until the end of your days. And when you are "old," you should also have the necessary mental tools to take responsibility for your own well-being. So why not ensure that your time on earth, as long or as short as it may be, is filled with as much quality of life as possible for you? I have worked with a 72-year-old client on improving quality of life. There is no such thing as too old.

So what is meditation?

If I was to describe meditation in a few words, I would choose the following adjectives: meditation is recuperative, uplifting, relentless, cleansing and enriching in every way.

Of course there are probably just as many answers to "What is meditation?" as there are people meditating in the world. After all, meditation is an individual, personal experience. But one thing is for sure, meditation is so much more than just a method of relaxation. Meditation as I understand it and the meditation I teach is about interacting with yourself. The unclouded contact with your inner being—sinking into yourself.

The good news is: you can trigger this sinking process yourself. The bad news is: *only* you can trigger this sinking process. In other words, it is up to you and you alone. This requires responsibility and fosters responsibility in equal measure. It is a process which demands concentration and also promotes concentration. Only the inner focus on the here and now turns purely sitting around into meditation.

There are numerous very different forms of meditation which can help you to achieve this. These range from conventional sitting methods and peaceful walking meditations to active forms of meditation with dance and shouting. Some forms of meditation actively involve the body, the voice, nature or objects, while others focus solely on the mind.

This wide range of methods allows us to select the most suitable meditation for our stage of life and level of experience, and enables us to practice until it is time for a change (either internally or physically). Meditation changes you, and you change your meditation.

Meditation is a process which constantly reveals new things over the course of years. Just as you are unable to play an instrument straight away after reading a music book, you are not yet able to meditate perfectly straight after reading a meditation book.

Though gods, angels and energy are not part of my reality, meditation is open for all kinds of spiritual beliefs. The type of meditation which I teach is independent of any confessional or esoteric concepts, so please feel free to integrate your own beliefs. I am offering you a foundation, you decide on how you make it grow. Everyone may integrate their own beliefs into their everyday life, their thoughts, actions or meditation to the extent that they feel comfortable. If religion provides you with inner peace and security, then you can integrate it into your meditation.

Keep your meditation as pure and authentic as you are. That is one of the great freedoms in our Aspie lives—to be who you are without having to adjust and cater to other needs.

Meditation is about you and nothing else. It is about doing. Simply doing. Meditating. You already have everything you need to start meditating: you.

This is the approach to meditation that I believe in and practice.

I teach Highmat® Meditation, which comes from the German word "Heimat" meaning "home." Do you want to get to know your inner home? Do you want to learn new things about yourself? Do you want to meditate, but don't know how? Do you want to bring your meditation up to a new level? Okay, then let's do it!

Chapter 2

The Benefits of Meditation for People with Asperger Syndrome

What is meditation generally good for?

One of my clients once summed it up perfectly: "Meditation is like a short holiday. You switch off your mind and afterwards you've completely recharged your batteries!"

It is scientifically proven that your heartbeat slows down during meditation, your breathing deepens and your muscles relax. It lowers your blood pressure, reduces stress, supports emotional processes and generally boosts your well-being. It goes without saying that these results are subjective and vary for every person practicing meditation and each different type of meditation.

The physical advantages and sensitized bodily perception should however only be a secondary motivation to start meditating. These should be seen as something akin to a positive bonus. Instead, the desire to switch off and enjoy peace and balance should take center stage. This longing for inner peace is the reason why most people start meditating, and I'm no exception to that.

The space for inner peace is offered by the fact that meditation means only doing one thing at a time. You solely focus on what you decide for yourself, your breath, your body, your inner self. You don't have to think about what's coming next, as the procedure is fixed and there is no need for variation. In a way, it's the polar opposite of multi-tasking—you could even call it single-tasking!

You can completely let go because during the meditation you are supported by the floor, chair, grass, your body and your mind. There is an inner and outer space surrounding your meditation where you can make things very comfortable. You can pass on your weight and leave tension behind.

This physical peace paves the way to the next step in meditation practice: inner contact with yourself. You can discover who you really are when the penetrating twitter of the mind can finally be ignored.

Centering yourself inwardly allows honest communication with your inner self, enabling deep insights. This allows you access to your own emotions. In this phase, a meditation is successful if the meditating person discovers something new about himself or herself during practice. Here, meditation becomes a judgment-free space. Nothing about yourself is bad or wrong, everything is simply what it is. You're absolutely perfect the way you are.

The advantage compared to other types of self-discovery and therefore the strength of meditation is that it does not require any aids and can be practiced anywhere without further ado. In addition, there is the road to this experience, which teaches you concentration, perseverance, hope, patience and assertiveness. All of these attributes form a stable foundation for mental health, confidence and an independent life.

My top 15 reasons to meditate

Meditation:

1. improves your health
2. improves the perception of your body
3. improves your concentration
4. improves your perseverance
5. improves your assertiveness
6. improves your patience
7. improves your sense of hope
8. improves your physical relaxation
9. improves your mental relaxation
10. improves inner communication
11. improves your tolerance
12. improves your access to your own feelings
13. improves your self-awareness
14. does not require any aids or outside help
15. can be practiced anywhere at any time.

Why is meditation especially good for Aspies?

Now you know why meditation is an excellent activity for everyone, so I'd next like to go into a little more detail about why meditation is especially worthwhile for Aspies.

Let me be honest with you from the outset—your life will not suddenly become "normal" through meditation. However, it might just become a bit more normal as it will equip you with the ability to deal more calmly with stimuli. In general, people with Asperger Syndrome are very sensitive to the stimuli around them. Visual, acoustic, haptic or olfactory input, as well as moods and vibrations of other people for some Aspies, are perceived much more sensitively than by neurotypicals (NTs).[1] This high sensitivity can quickly lead to sensory overload, which builds inner stress and in the worst case scenario leads to psychological breakdown (meltdown).

A breakdown like this is a very exhausting, frightening and threatening experience which leaves you with a sense of helplessness and surrender, and of being different. These effects are felt by the people directly affected and those around them. In order to prevent dramatic breakdowns such as these, you need the ability to estimate your body's own boundaries, a good knowledge of your own feelings and limits, a sense of your own needs and the skill to implement these insights into practicable plans. In a world full of incalculable factors, it is often not possible to successfully implement prevention measures.

The best way to prevent meltdowns is often a mix of different factors, with meditation being one reliable and effective method in the long term. Meditation is well-suited to this for a number of reasons: on the one hand, your inner perception becomes more sensitive, both in physical and mental respects. You gain the ability to differentiate between feelings: this allows you to identify your personal physical and mental signals of an impending meltdown at an earlier stage and therefore enables you to take countermeasures in good time.

On the other hand, by working with yourself during meditation, you can develop new strategies for how to deal

---

1   The term neurotypical describes a person with typical neurological development, i.e. the majority of people, and is often used by the autistic community to describe people who are not on the autism spectrum.

with yourself, your perception and your feelings. Over time, you will become more secure and confident in dealing with your emotions, even in stressful situations. In this way, you can gain new solutions which give you the chance to react in the best way possible during a breakdown.

As I mentioned earlier I have suffered from anxieties for many years of my life; I call the result of this experience "I know fear in all its guises." I know big, paralyzing fears that include everything that surrounds you. And I know small, subtle fears that go directly on specific situations in one's daily life.

Those years have been very tiring, as on a regular basis every night I had to cry because of fear. One of the methods my therapist has developed with me was based on meditation. Those were the first steps into walking meditation for me, just walking up and down in my room, feeling my soles, feeling my breath, getting a feeling of my body and my surroundings; to escape from my head and its web of fears. As I slowly mastered the meditation, I slowly mastered my fear.

Meditation is helpful to deal with anxieties because it helps to move the awareness from the fear to the present. It moves the awareness from the outside—where the fear comes from—to the inside, where you can decide what to do. It helps to focus on your breathing in a situation where you thought you can't breathe because of fear. Meditation gives you a secure environment in a situation where you think you have lost all security.

So you see that in addition, the more you meditate, the more balanced and calm you will feel, which is a very good prerequisite for ensuring meltdowns occur less regularly.

Calmness naturally helps in other stressful everyday situations, such as bullying, worries, boredom and feelings of exclusion.

Increased sensitivity and a deeper understanding of your inner processes allow you to develop a different perception and understanding of yourself. You become more familiar with your feelings and begin to understand them. This strengthens your image of yourself and you gain an insight into who you actually are.

This self-discovery might be something that NTs like to think about, or not. They fit into society, feel part of it and don't need much effort to find their place in life. Some people give this more attention than others, although many address it after suffering a crisis. In contrast, for you as an Aspie, someone who hasn't fit into the norms of society since birth, self-awareness is a must for a stable psyche and necessary for a clear understanding of who you are. This image of yourself is a combination of how others perceive you, how you perceive yourself, your opinion of yourself and to what extent you can accept the way you are.

Knowing your own value, your own assessment and your own perception of yourself as a person with Asperger Syndrome in our society is an essential component of living a self-determined, satisfied life.

Another positive way in which meditation can improve your life: the better you know your own feelings, the better you will recognize those of others and be able to deal with them. It goes without saying that it is difficult to be aware of the feelings of others if you don't know these feelings from your own experience, or at least don't have a feel for the nuances and names of these feelings. Meditation, focusing on yourself inwardly, opens new access to your feelings. It allows you to get to know yourself and your feelings in peace and in a safe environment. This will facilitate your interaction with other people for the rest of your life, make daily interactions at school or in a professional environment easier, as well as friendships, family and romantic relationships.

I don't want to neglect the topic of bodies. Many Aspies have coordination deficits, are somewhat clumsy or have problems with bodily processes. Meditation can be a big help in training your own perception of your body. This is a gentle holistic method which allows you to carefully discover your body from the inside out.

When you meditate, you don't need to ask yourself "What do they want from me?" The question is in fact: "What do I want from me?" What do you want to achieve for yourself personally? Relaxation? Independence? Getting to know yourself? Dealing with yourself? Improving your quality of life? Your goal is the focus here.

By meditating, you are doing something for yourself. You take care of yourself and create the basis for an independent life.

Why Aspies are good at meditation

You've heard lots of good reasons why you *should* meditate as an Aspie. Now it's time to outline why you *can* meditate particularly well as an Aspie.

Meditation requires devotion. It is a long-term activity which you have to practice with patience and regularity in order to master and use it effectively. It requires long-term effort and commitment. This is a prerequisite that many Aspies already have, and which they channel in the form of specialist knowledge or areas of interest which they devote a great deal of attention to.

Ritual forms the backbone of meditation. The practice contains set processes, and there are also set elements surrounding meditation which you can make part of your ritual. The security offered by meditation can equip you with trust, freedom and relaxation. Why? Because you don't have to devote any thoughts to the exterior. When you meditate, everything is defined and adjusted to your individual needs. You can throw yourself into the ritual and completely give yourself over to the experience.

Meditation is individual work. You don't need anyone else to do it. You don't have to integrate anyone else and you don't need to communicate with anyone else. To meditate, you are not forced to interpret anyone's behavior and you don't have to make yourself clear to anyone. Experiencing solitude here does not make you a crank, in fact introverted thought is an essential prerequisite for meditation. Groups are not necessary, but even in meditation groups interaction is reduced to a minimum.

Meditation requires focus. During meditation, only one thing is in focus. It might be your breathing, your body, your movements or your inner self. You can ignore everything else. You can let all the details go and focus your concentration solely on your goal, just as you can with your favorite hobby.

The ability to perceive many details, which is possessed by many Aspies including myself, also helps in perceiving your own body and feelings. Combined with concentration, this is an effective method for communicating with yourself—for meditation.

Meditation requires honesty. One of the criticisms often expressed towards Aspies is that we are too honest, that we take things too literally and that we communicate with our surroundings in an unfiltered way. Honesty is an essential part of meditation. If you are not honest when communicating with yourself, you will never be able to change anything. It goes without saying that not everything which you discover within will be pleasant. But if you don't want to face unpleasant feelings in the first place, you will never be able to change. Taking an honest look at yourself offers you the chance to change.

Meditation is effective in combination with images. Many Aspies tend to understand statements and terms too literally, which can quickly lead to misunderstandings and problems in daily communication. But when it comes to looking within, it is often helpful to take things "too literally." Meditation images such as "You are an empty vessel" can have a powerful emotional effect, especially if you find it easy to visualize such images in your mind.

You can find out more about which meditations are suitable for which aspects of your Asperger Syndrome in the section on "Forms of meditation and Aspie characteristics" in Chapter 6.

As you can see, as an Aspie you already have a lot of characteristics which facilitate the art of meditation. In turn, meditation can give a lot to you as an Aspie, making your life easier in the long run.

My top 15 advantages of meditation for Aspies

Meditation:

1. helps to prevent meltdowns

2. helps in stressful situations, e.g. meltdowns

3. reduces the frequency of meltdowns

4. improves the perception of your body

5. improves self-awareness and the sense of your place in the world

6. improves your physical relaxation

7. improves your mental relaxation

8. improves access to your own feelings

9. facilitates interaction with others

10. does not require any aids or external help

11. requires an introverted approach

12. requires concentration

13. requires long-term devotion

14. requires attention to detail

15. requires honesty.

Chapter 3

Motivation to Meditate

One of the recurring themes in my work is motivation. And because meditation is a technique which requires a great deal of devotion, it is certainly important to be sufficiently motivated. So before we look any deeper into the topic of meditation, I would first like to touch on motivation in this chapter.

The fact is that nobody can be forced to meditate if they don't want to. You would simply sit there during the meditation time and resign yourself to this activity without opening your consciousness up to a new experience.

It is therefore vital that you have some basic motivation which you can build on. The previous chapter maybe gave you some arguments which form the basis of motivation, as I listed many points which speak in favor of meditation for everybody and Aspies in particular. Here are some tips to ensure meditation is successful in the long term.

Tips to stay motivated
Make a decision
Make a conscious decision to want to meditate. This is made internally. It shouldn't take long, but it does require conviction. The decision should then be implemented by

you as a responsible, mature person—with continuity, decisiveness, patience and hope.

Seek support

As you know, not all Aspies are introverted loners. If you are an Aspie with a support network around you—either real world or virtual—then seek support among them. Tell everybody that you will be meditating from now on and ask them to support you in this. For instance, you could ask them to help motivate you to meditate when you are finding it difficult to motivate yourself. In addition, you may find it more difficult to give up your plan if you've already told a lot of people, resulting in positive social pressure.

Set realistic goals

Set yourself realistic goals. It is very unrealistic to expect the feeling of sinking into yourself, enjoying a peaceful mind and serenity after just a couple of meditation sessions.

In meditation, timescales are somewhat longer. When it comes to the results of meditation, don't count hours or days, count the months or even years. If you set yourself the goal of having positive meditation experiences within one year, you are much more likely to achieve your goal than if you only give yourself one or two months.

Practice "dry training"

As part of my swimming training as a child, I had to take part in so-called "dry training." In other words, it was swimming training without water, in which muscles would be exercised on machines, stretched and physical conditioning generally improved. It was preparation for the actual action of swimming. When it comes to meditation, you can do something similar using the tips in Chapter 5: "Welcoming Meditation into Your

Everyday Life." This ensures that you are always "in training" even if you are not directly meditating. Meditation remains in your mind, which in turn reduces the danger that you lose the motivation to meditate. And as you are already going to the effort of doing "dry training," it wouldn't make any sense not to turn this success into real meditation. What's more, everyday practice will help you achieve positive results quicker, which is certainly a motivation to continue.

List the long-term benefits

Write yourself a list with two columns, for advantages and disadvantages. On the advantage side, write the benefits or positive effects that you expect if you continue to meditate regularly, for example more inner balance. On the disadvantage side, write the benefits or positive effects if you do not continue to meditate, for example more time to read.

Pool these pro and con arguments under groups of time: what is the benefit in two hours? What is it in two days? In two weeks? Two months? Two years? Twenty years?

You can also rate the individual arguments. Perhaps you can give them a points score from 1 (very weak) to 10 (very strong). How much is leading a more balanced life worth to you? Quite a lot? Maybe 8 points. And how important is it to you to have one more hour to read? It certainly wouldn't hurt. Maybe 6 points. You therefore have 8 points on the pro side and 6 points on the con side.

As you decided to take up meditation in the first place, you have to expect that the pro side will outweigh the con side in the end. If you then have a problem with motivation, get out the list and remind yourself of why you decided to start meditating in the first place. This can give you fresh impetus to carry on, even at a time when you have your doubts.

If your list of cons outweighs the list of pros, then you perhaps need to rethink your decision to start meditating.

If you can't think of any more pro arguments in the days that follow, then perhaps meditation is not something for you. Or you could simply give it a try despite all the lists and simply concentrate on the act of meditating.

Use visualization

Many professional sports people use visualization methods to achieve their goals. This is easier said than done, but it is a very effective method: imagine how you would feel if the meditation provides long-term successes. Imagine it as visually, haptically and emotionally as possible. If you meditate successfully in the long term, how will you feel in peaceful situations such as everyday life? How you feel in stressful periods? Your list of advantages may be helpful here.

Set up a reward system

We all love receiving praise and rewards. Why not use this natural evolutionary bonus and set up your own reward system. You can draw a star in your calendar on every day when you meditate as planned and then reward yourself at the end of every month according to the number of stars you've drawn. Did you manage a whole month? Then treat yourself to a huge bowl of ice cream with all the trimmings. Achieved 70 percent stars? Treat yourself to three scoops with chocolate shavings. Define your own scale and tailor it to your preferences. I'm sure you can think of some small luxury which would boost your motivation.

Draw on your meditation experiences

If you've already had some positive meditation experiences, make them visible. Write them down, paint them or draw them. Visualize and note down everything that you can remember or if you keep a meditation book, read it.

And—just like with the list of advantages—whenever you are finding it difficult to motivate yourself, take a moment to look at your positive experiences. That is surely enough to equip you with the motivation to continue meditating.

Chapter 4

Mind, Body, Soul and Emotions

What to Expect When You Meditate

Meditation and emotions

Meditation can stir up a lot of emotions. These can be positive emotions such as happiness, carefreeness and peace. However, it can also bring about negative emotions such as sadness, anger and loneliness. But don't worry, in my experience the subconscious regulates the intensity of your emotions effectively—you only experience the difficult emotions in doses that you are able to deal with them.

Perhaps you are now saying to yourself: "I thought that meditation was supposed to calm me down! How can I be calm if meditation is stirring up fear inside me?!" That's a good question, so please allow me to explain.

As you may have already read, I see meditation as a long-term method, something which requires patience in order to reap the benefits in the long term. You therefore also need some patience to become a calmer and more balanced person. In addition, achieving calmness and balance requires a better understanding of your own feelings. But what does "a better understanding" actually mean?

We all, whether Aspies or NTs, experience emotions which are undesirable and which may be unpleasant for us.

Meditation gives you the chance to open yourself to the feelings which you might otherwise shut out. In everyday life, we are often very successful in suppressing these unpleasant emotions and keeping a lid on things, allowing us to master the challenges of everyday life. However, when we escape the hubbub and take time for ourselves, such as during meditation, the artificial barriers holding back shunned emotions start to crumble.

You could compare it to a boiling pot of stew: you hold these emotions hidden inside you—keeping a lid on them so to speak. When you cover these emotions, pressure starts to build in the pot, it begins to boil and the lid becomes unstable. However, if you briefly take off the lid and allow a few of your emotions out, the pressure is reduced and things continue to cook in a much calmer way. So from this point of view, setting these emotions free is a positive, desirable and healthy effect of meditation.

The more often and longer you have the confidence to give these unpleasant emotions some space, the less intensively you will suffer as a result of them.

I have the following tip for dealing with feelings like these which occur during meditation: make a deal with yourself. Allow yourself, for example, to experience these feelings for five minutes. Or one minute, fifteen minutes, or only just a few seconds. Then place the lid back on top of them, shift your concentration back to your body, your breathing or positive feelings and continue your meditation as planned.

If these emotions become too much for you, then end the meditation, write down what was going through your head or distract yourself, go out, spend some time doing something you enjoy, such as reading a good book or stroking your dog.

Whatever the case, don't forget to be proud of yourself if you were courageous enough to allow pent-up emotions out. This requires courage, assertiveness and honesty towards yourself. It is a great step towards taking your life into your own hands!

The benefits of meditation often appear in subtle ways, for example confronting your emotions gradually bears fruit, but this happens slowly and to such an extent that you may not even consciously notice that something has changed. Reviewing your feelings in an honest, open way at monthly intervals is therefore just as helpful as writing a diary or meditation book.

Meditation and mind

A farmer is working in his fields. On the horizon, he sees a big cloud of dust coming his way. He stands up, wipes the sweat from his brow and shields his eyes from the sun in order to get a better look at the dust cloud. The cloud gradually draws nearer and the farmer notices that the dust is being kicked up by rider on a horse galloping at full speed along the path next to his field. "Where are you going in such a hurry?" calls the farmer to the rider as soon as he is within earshot. "I don't know!" replies the rider who seems a little uncertain on his steed. "Ask the horse!"

This short story which I heard first on a public presentation with the Buddhist monk Thich Nhat Hanh (1998) might put a smile on your face because it should really be the rider telling the horse where to go and how fast. The rider should be able to master the horse.

Why am I telling you this story? Because you should be able to master your mind. Master your thoughts. Master the thoughts which go through your head, when and to what intensity.

But we all, whether Aspies or not, know situations in which we are anything but masters of our own mind.

These might be peaceful situations, such as when we are lying in bed at night and can't get thoughts out of our head. Perhaps we are thinking about things that have happened during the day—unsolved problems, unspoken thoughts, hidden desires, fears or plans for the next day. It could be stressful situations in which we are bombarded with so many thoughts at once that we have chaos in our head, which only slowly subsides.

One aim of meditation is to calm the thoughts in our head—just like the horse. The aim is not to control the thoughts, as control always suggests some form of repression with effort and dominance. It is much more to do with the ability to calm your thoughts. To slow them down. To give yourself some time out. Allowing peace to rule your mind.

It may sound somewhat crazy, but the following technique helped me when I was learning this. I thanked my mind: "Thank you that you work so hard for me and that you help me think." And I then allowed it freedom: "But right now I don't need you. You can just take it easy. I will let you know when I need you again."

After hearing the story about the rider and the horse, I imagined each one of my thoughts as a horse from the story. And then I calmed every horse down, slowing them from a gallop to a trot, from a trot to standstill, simply by imagining the image of the horse in my mind and how it slows down. To do this, I didn't even need to know what the specific thought was. Thanks to this inner communication and these images in my mind, I found it easier to calm the stream of thoughts in my head.

It is vital to give your thoughts some freedom for creativity and solving problems. The best ideas come to us when we think intensively about a problem and then are able to let it go within our thoughts and "sleep on it." The brain then has time to conceive solutions and ideas using pathways and synaptic connections which we could never have consciously drawn on. As a result, creativity requires space, time and peace for the solution. Meditation can give you all three. Inner space, time to yourself and peace for the mind.

Meditation and body

Scientific studies have, as we have seen, proven that meditation has positive effects on the body (for example, Murphy and Donovan 1997). Your heartbeat slows down during meditation, your breathing deepens and muscle tension is reduced. It lowers your blood pressure, reduces stress, supports emotional processes and generally boosts your well-being. It goes without saying that these results are subjective and are different for every person practicing meditation and type of meditation.

Peaceful forms of physical activity such as yoga, Tai Chi or Qigong are associated with and practiced in a way which is mentally and practically synonymous with meditation.

The fact that the body can also be challenged during the act of meditation is an aspect that is often overlooked, or indeed completely unknown.

There are a range of active meditation forms in which the body is consciously used to attain a meditation experience (for more on this see Chapter 6: "Different Forms of Meditation"). Consciousness of the body is also part of effective meditation in its passive forms, the majority of which are practiced in the sitting position.

If you have any physical impairments, stay within your boundaries. If you tend to suffer from back pain, passive sitting meditation or active meditation involving jumping are perhaps not appropriate for you. Exercise common sense with your body and listen to it when selecting which meditation form is most suitable for you and which does you most good.

There are also types of meditation which propagate "overcoming the body," such as sitting for so long in uncomfortable positions until you no longer feel the pain or no longer attempt to fight it. The intention is to direct your concentration completely towards the mind, in this way achieving mental enlightenment and rising above the human and physical level. I don't believe in this. Especially not for beginners. If you simply want to meditate, there is no point in punishing yourself physically.

In the modern world, where in the West only a few people still have to work physically, the perception of body is a commonly forgotten topic at the best of times. Working at a computer, in the aisles of the supermarket, an evening in front of the TV or sitting in bed with a good book do not place any great challenges on our body and they do not require any special perception of our own body from our point of view. Consciously perceiving our own body is something that is lost in everyday life; the body has to function or be healed with medicine.

Therefore perhaps including the body in our awareness is a key prerequisite to achieving a better life. The first step is to come to the realization that the body leads us through life on a day-to-day basis. What a gift it can be when we consciously perceive our body and care for it.

Breema Bodywork® has helped me a great deal in this respect. One of its principles is "body is comfortable." The fact that I am allowed to make myself comfortable was an experience in itself. Not only in meditation courses and self-healing seminars where you would sit on the floor, but also in everyday situations, the subway, on the sofa, in the shower, carrying shopping, even when you're stroking the cat. I began to ask myself more and more whether I couldn't make my body even more comfortable. Most of the time, the answer was "Yes!" and so I made myself even more comfortable.

I apply this principle in meditation and I would encourage you to make yourself comfortable when you meditate, even if instructions online tell you that your back has to be perfectly straight and that certain fingers have to be touching so that the energy flows correctly. Your posture doesn't matter—irrespective of what is taught. You can stand, sit, lie down, you can even fall asleep during meditation! Although this isn't the purpose of meditation, it doesn't do any harm and who would ever speak out against a recuperating nap?

You can of course try out meditating and sitting according to fixed rules. Maybe it provides you with the structure that you need to let go. Perhaps these boundaries give you the experience that you are looking for. Perhaps these pains give you a conscious appreciation of what you need.

But please do this voluntarily because you have chosen to yourself, not because it is written in a book.

Your meditation experiences are not impacted by you holding a particular position. You alone are responsible for yourself and if you don't ensure that you feel comfortable in your own body, then no one else will. As I have repeated several times, meditation is a process which requires personal responsibility, so take this responsibility and take care of your physical well-being.

Body meditations

There is no *definitive* body meditation. There are all sorts of methods, forms, physical exercises and techniques which could be called body meditation. In general, these are certain sequences of movements and poses which can help aid meditation. How does a sequence of movements become body meditation? Simply by your making it into meditation with your inner mindset. You can do this in exactly the same way as how you turn sitting on the ground into meditation through your thoughts. The power of your thoughts can turn ritualized movements into meditation. Cool, isn't it? Just like Yoda!

There are numerous well-known forms of physical exercise which can serve as the basis for meditation, such as Tai Chi, Qigong and the sun salutation from the yoga tradition. Here I want to present a lesser-known physical exercise because I think it is extraordinarily well suited to this: Breema Bodywork® and in this case, Self Breema® in particular.

The people at Breema are very particular about what they allow others to write about them. Therefore I would like to stress that the following paragraph is *my* opinion. I'm giving you my lowdown on Breema as I have experienced it.

To me, Breema is a type of meditation packaged in bodywork form. The fantastic and liberating thing about Breema is that everything is allowed and is correct as long as you do it with your full attention and commitment. As a result, Breema makes it insignificant whether you have handicap or if you're missing an arm, if you are allergic to certain things or indeed if you are an Aspie. That also means that if you forget which movement comes next in the Breema sequence, you simply carry on and do what you can remember and it is fine.

I used to suffer considerably due to my strong sense of perfectionism and this made my life very tiring. The freedom offered by Breema was very liberating to me. You don't have to do it perfectly for it to work. You can simply do it as well as you can.

As mentioned above, another Breema principle is that your body should be comfortable at all times. I will come back to this at various points during this book because this concept alone can improve your quality of life. Especially in today's world, I see a thought like this as vitally important and necessary.

Breema has other principles which stand out due to their simplicity but nevertheless help make your life more harmonious. Over and above these principles, Breema is primarily a bodywork technique—you work with your body when you do it. But don't worry, it's not tiring.

The type of touch which takes place during Breema is different to what we're used to in everyday life. In general, people always intend something when they touch; they touch to make contact, to express tenderness, to turn someone on, to keep someone at arm's length, whatever.

With Breema, you simply touch because the other person is there. The body of another person offers the opportunity to perceive your own body. Experiencing this form of unconditional touch, either with another person or on my own, was a revelation to me at the time and very liberating, healing, nourishing, present but still anonymous.

Conventional Breema takes place between two people: one person who gives and another who receives, although the boundaries here are very flexible. If you are curious about this type of interpersonal touch, you could book a Breema session yourself and try it out.

As physical contact is not exactly something that most Aspies search for and is also something which always requires a willing partner, I'm going to concentrate on Self Breema here.

Self Breema, as the name suggests, is done on your own. Self Breema consists of a range of small sequences. One sequence is a pattern of touches and movements. As the sequence is pre-defined, you can completely relax and you do not have to think about what to do next. You can completely let go and let your mind be blank. Select a sequence which you like. Carry out the sequence with unconditional touch and total commitment.

For a full selection of Self Breema sequences, I recommend the corresponding book or seminars (see "Useful Resources"). For more information on Breema please visit the website www.breema.com.

My personal recommendation: carry out the sequence over and over again until your meditation time is over. This repeated exercise provides security, peace and presence.

As a precursor to experiencing and learning about the technique, you might just touch your leg with your hand. Not with a view to achieving anything or wanting to achieve anything, or having to achieve anything, simply because your hand is there and your leg is there. You want to feel how your leg feels in that moment. You want to feel with your leg how your hand feels in that moment. Get your mind involved, allow it to describe what you are doing.

How is this beneficial? You focus your thoughts, you shift your attention to your body and you move into the here and now. In short, you are present. An outstanding basis for meditation.

Meditation and the soul

Nobody can really say what the soul actually is. I therefore always had problems with this term as it was simply too abstract for me. Nevertheless, I would like to say that meditation is good for the soul—whatever that may be.

For me, it means that meditation does me good. It helps me be a calm and balanced person. I feel nourished, strengthened and personally equipped for the challenges and strain of everyday life through meditation.

The soul is also a term used in spiritual and mental health. This aspect of health also suffers in the case of modern stress-related disorders such as depression or burnout, which bring this aspect of the body out of balance. Our society, which is built on functioning and performance, neglects this aspect of everyday life so that measures are only offered—or indeed sought—when it is already too late; depression has already begun and burnout can clearly be felt.

In today's fast moving world, in which depression, exhaustion and burnout are everyday words, meditation is gaining a new status as a gentle, low-cost and long-term measure for combating the side effects of working life. Aspies often feel an even greater pressure as they are able to perceive more than most people with their senses. We often find social pressure more difficult to deal with and also find family and financial situations challenging due to our Aspie traits.

In German there is a saying which roughly translates as "set the soul free" or perhaps "hang loose" in English. It means relax, let tension go, consciously do nothing, at least nothing which requires effort. Meditation is ideal for this. It allows you to put the trials of everyday life to one side. Not having to conform to any rules, not having to communicate, not having to read any messages or report to anybody.

I'm not saying that meditation will solve all the problems on earth or that it is the gateway to being happy for the rest of your life. There are always multiple factors which play a role in healing illnesses, or enjoying happiness. However, meditation can play a major part in this. It is one solution of many which helps you to maintain your personal health and soul, for a happier life.

Chapter 5

Welcoming Meditation into Your Everyday Life

Exercises for everyday life

There are a whole host of different methods to support your meditation practice in everyday life and aid you in remembering your meditation experiences during stressful situations in order to relax. I've put a few suggestions together for you here.

Practicing concentration

If you would like to practice focusing your mind and thoughts—on something other than your favorite hobby—then I suggest trying the following preparation for meditation: Look for an object of your choice. This may be a vase, a shoe, a computer, a dice, an orange, your cat or so forth.

Then sit in front of your object and simply observe it in a concentrated manner for half an hour. Perceive every detail, every corner, every contour, the quality of the surfaces, the light against the surfaces, the shadows, the different shades and colors—in short, everything that you can see.

Repeat the exercise on the following day. You could try again with the same object, from the same perspective (I admit that this is difficult in the case of a cat) and start observing it all over again. This requires continuity but may surprise you with all the new things you discover. Does it look different today? Do the colors seem different? What about the light?

Or you could change your perspective, turn the object a little and start observing it again.

If this seems too boring for you initially, select a new object and focus on it until you develop the stamina to spend time with one and the same object.

Relaxation methods

Learn a relaxation method. Methods such as autogenic training or progressive muscle relaxation can be learned quickly. You don't even have to attend a course to do this, simply purchase a few good CDs with instructions (see "Useful Resources"). By using a different method of relaxation, you will facilitate your introduction to meditation.

Guided imagery

Guided imagery is another great way of taking your first steps in meditation. Guided images are short stories which aim to relax mind and body.

If it comes easily to you to imagine things that you hear, if you enjoy creating pictures of what you hear or read in your head, and can easily create images in your mind's eye this approach is suitable for you. There are numerous books and CDs which serve as inspiration for guided imagery (see "Useful Resources").

Short breaks

Everyday life offers plenty of opportunities for quick breathers, if only we knew how to use them. For instance, every time the telephone rings, you have the opportunity to breathe deeply right into your belly before you pick up the phone and start the conversation. Or before you open an email. When you're standing in the queue at the supermarket, waiting for the bus or at a traffic light. There are so many opportunities to integrate relaxation into everyday life.

Images

Why proceed according to instructions? You can use images in numerous situations for meditation: watching trains, standing on a bridge over the motorway, following the flight of birds or the passing of clouds, the soft swaying of a corn field, trees or waves, looking at strings of numbers, admiring your favorite painting, watching a screensaver or putting a jigsaw puzzle together. Personally, I like looking at the numbers of my authenticator, or at my sleeping pets or getting stuck into a number puzzle.

Enjoyment box

Look for a few things that you like. Perhaps these things simply make you laugh or bring you joy. Gather a few together and then place them all in a box. It may only be a photo or a memory written down. This simple method gives you the opportunity to pull a great feeling "out of the box" at any time.

Happiness diary

Every evening, take a notebook and write down three things which you liked that day, which put a smile on your face and made you laugh. It might be something unusual, such as an unexpected gift, perhaps something more abstract, such as the taste of cornflakes, or something quite normal but nevertheless beautiful, such as the sunshine in the early morning.

Do you feel like you didn't have anything to laugh about? I've endured a lot of tough years when I was depressive but I still found three things to write, even in the darkest days. I'm sure that you can too!

Meditation book

When you have started writing a meditation book (see Chapter 8: "Aids for Meditation"), you can always carry this with you, allowing you to read inside and remember the feelings you took from the meditation. This can make phases of psychological stress easier to cope with.

Nourishing TV

Or how about a little TV? I'm not talking about senseless channel hopping. I'm talking about specific DVDs which relax you, such as the BBC documentary film series *Planet Earth* (my advice: put it on mute), *Earth from Above*, ballet performances, the world's most beautiful train journeys or simply a DVD showing an open fire or an aquarium scene— whatever relaxes you best (see "Useful Resources").

Nourishing exercise

Include your body in your meditation. Physical exercises such as yoga, Tai Chi, Qigong, the Feldenkrais method (see "Useful Resources") or swimming, golf, rowing and similar sports are great accompaniments to meditation. These calming methods of physical exertion are intended to connect body, mind and soul, using the body to look inwards.

The meditation ritual

As you would expect, through regular practice, meditation automatically becomes a ritual over time. Particularly among us Aspies, ritual provides orientation, security and is a calming influence in this confusing and over-stimulating world. In my life I learned that rituals are helpful in everyday life. Rituals allow you to actively strive for a better life. By consciously adding positive rituals into your routine, you can have a greater influence over yourself and your life in general. It's no coincidence that professional sports people work with rituals in order to deliver top performance in high-pressure situations. As you can see, even if rituals had only provided inner security up to now, there are other good reasons to add rituals to your life.

If you would like to make a ritual out of your meditation practice, the security it provides is not the only benefit. It also helps your subconscious prepare itself for the feeling of meditation at the start of the ritual, which, over time, serves to make it easier to relax. If you have developed a feel for how you perceive meditation, individual elements of the ritual can trigger these inner experiences, allowing you to benefit from them more easily.

The meditation ritual can consist of many individual elements. It starts with the time and place which you select for the meditation. Then it continues with the clothing that you choose. A certain type of music—only to get you in the mood or during the meditation itself—or the lighting of a candle can initiate the start of meditation time. One of my clients always read a certain fable to start her daily meditation, as this story has calmed down since her childhood days and it now signals that her meditation is beginning—a time for herself. Another client began every meditation with a vanilla cookie, because the taste calmed her down, left her feeling protected and gave her a sense of peace.

Just as an element of the ritual can signal the start of meditation practice, you can also include an element which heralds the end. This might be the gong sound of a meditation alarm, the systematic stretching of all limbs or a gulp of your favorite fruit juice.

Rituals are nourishing. Meditation is nourishing. Nourish yourself and your soul with planned, ritualized actions which put you in contact with your inner self.

Some of this may sound odd to you. You might ask yourself: how can it help me to learn meditating when I watch TV? Or stick nice things in a box? That may sound a bit far off, I admit, but it does make sense. With including these new habits into your life you give a signal to yourself, your mind, your consciousness, that you are ready for a change—even though it may be subtle in the beginning. You include a habit that focuses on something nice, something calm, something nourishing for your soul. You don't have to think of anything, don't have to answer or respond to someone. You open an inner room where you can be yourself. And that is the same inner room your meditation takes place in. So these habits may help you to get to know your private inner space, to feel comfortable there on a daily basis—to make it part of your daily ritual.

Chapter 6

Different Forms of Meditation

There are numerous forms and methods of meditation. In simple terms, they can be divided into active and passive meditation.

In the case of active meditation, participants move around. These meditations are often divided into various phases, in which the type of movement changes.

In the case of passive meditation, the body is still, without moving or only making very few movements. One well-known type of passive meditation is silent meditation, in which the participants are not to speak, sing or hum.

However, this difference only describes the body. In every type of meditation, the mind is supposed to be active but at the same time quiet.

Selecting a meditation form

To start with, I recommend selecting the type of meditation which most appeals to you. In this chapter, you will find information which helps you to make the choice.

One tip in advance of any decision-making: I often recommend that beginners avoid quiet and silent meditations to begin with because this form poses the greatest challenge and is therefore often associated with disappointment when no rapid successes are achieved. For beginners, active meditation is generally the better option because the mind can concentrate more easily on the movements.

Forms of meditation and Aspie characteristics

Before I present several forms of meditation in detail, I would first like to connect typical characteristics of Asperger Syndrome with types of meditation. You can find instructions for the meditations described here in the section on "Introduction to various forms of meditation" later in this chapter.

This overview of the combinations can make it easier for you to decide on one form.

Trouble switching off

If you find it difficult to relax, I advise starting with active meditation. In this form, the movement offers the mind some occupation, allowing it to be integrated constantly into the action and allowing you easy access to the meditation itself. I had huge problems in switching my babbling mind off, when I started meditation, and for years since. And I had, as probably do most meditation beginners, high expectations on the one hand on how a meditation should work—calming—and on the other hand how meditation is to be done—sitting around. So I was honestly baffled when I got introduced to active meditations in a seminar once. It opened a whole new meditation-world to me.

Attention to detail

Attention to detail is particularly predominant in the Vipassana meditation. Here, the focus is on looking inwards during the meditation, perceiving subtle signals from your body and thoughts, but not holding onto them or judging them. I have a particular love of detail too. When I walk on the street I spot out that one small safety pin someone has lost there or I detect that one pile on the floor of the public pool that doesn't match the others. Doing Vipassana meditation helped me to get more relaxed with those irregularities in life, even to appreciate them here and there.

Ritualized processes

Fixed, repeated rituals are part of many active meditations, which have various phases already predefined. The traditional Zazen meditation offers a good silent form, in which movement and processes are predefined, from correctly preparing the cushion to walking properly. I like the thought that the procedure of a meditation is pre-arranged. This way it is possible to completely let go of thoughts about how to go on, what to do next, as the procedure tells me how to go on and what to do next. I discovered Zen only late in my meditation career and had the courage to pick out those rituals that support me and let go of the rest. Adapt meditation to your rituals—not external rituals to your meditation.

Movements

There are many active meditations in which you can integrate your need or will to move. Many have phases dedicated to free movement, in the form of dance or fidgeting, depending on what your body feels like doing in that moment. I remember that as a child I had an inner urge to move that often made my Mom mad when I was expressing it—when we sat at the table for dinner, for example. Isn't it great that with active meditations you have an official permission to move, dance, jump around? Feel free to follow the needs of your body;

shift your awareness to your inner self and you will have an excellent meditation experience.

Spinning

Spinning movements can also be integrated into meditation. This can either take the form of a free movement in an active meditation or explicitly as a component of the whirling meditation. As spinning is a special kind of movement, the same goes here as for movements in general.

Problems with movement/bodily coordination

In order to train body perception but still meditate safely, I recommend the Vipassana meditation in this case, which promotes an inner journey in your body. As you might have read by now, meditation can be very challenging on a physical level. Safety comes first so don't feel obliged to start with a spectacular-looking active meditation. Choosing a subtle meditation form helps you to support your physical perception at the same time as meditating.

Repeating words

If you have words which you like to repeat as they offer security and relaxation, a peaceful mantra meditation comes highly recommended. Personally I find it very calming to repeat words and quickly became a friend of chanting mantras. Today it serves me as a useful tool to calm myself down in moments of distress; I either sing them aloud or inside my head.

Humming

If you tend to hum or make other noises, meditations involving sound would be suitable, such as the Nadabrahma or the mantra meditation. I tend to hum and sing for myself a lot during the day. Some people give me amused looks but I don't think anything of it—and keep on vocalizing. Meanwhile, after years of meditation and chanting, I often hum or sing mantras, which calms me down in a double way: first, because of the humming; second, because of the mantra words that are connected to a meditative state of mind for myself.

Mutism

Mutism can be a part of meditation. By the same token, meditation can help against mutism if you would like it to. I have known times when it has been so loud in my own head that I couldn't get a word out at all. I was afraid, disturbed and blocked. There were so many words inside me, too many at once that I couldn't decide what I should say, so I simply didn't say anything. In meditation, it's fine not to speak. You don't have to force yourself to want to say something. No one is hanging on your words. There is no one you have to communicate with. It's a relaxation zone, a haven of peace where you are allowed to remain mute. Particularly when it comes to excess noise in your head, the retreat to meditation can often help. From a personal point of view, phases of great stress which have kept me quiet have been diffused by meditation, allowing me to find my words and speak with an authentic voice.

If you tend to mutism, silent meditation, whether active or passive, can have a positive influence on phases of mutism as well as a relaxing and balancing effect overall.

Visual imagination

Meditation often involves working with images in the mind's eye. This may be relatively easy for you if you are able to take imaging instructions literally, for example imagine you are an empty vessel. In this case, I recommend the Vipassana meditation. Regarding visual imagination I am a typical Aspie. Everything I hear is mentally translated into visuals, especially expressions like "killing two birds with one stone" or "It's raining cats and dogs." What might be funny or even obstructive in daily life can be a great source of inspiration and focus when it comes to meditation. You may start a meditation with guided imagery, using your skill, to move over in a meditation and experience yourself with the help of images.

Artistic meditation

Aspies are often very creative! If you like to express yourself in artistic ways, meditating with mandalas is an excellent option. Through art we are capable of expressing thoughts and emotions that are often hard to explain with words. We use art as a bridge to communicate, not only with others we share our art with but especially with ourselves. Before a piece of art can be created we need an inner contact to what we want to express—and thus an inner connection is made. An inner dialogue can take place. And that is what meditation is about—an inner dialogue, without words, silent but intense.

Stick or switch?

At the beginning, I suggest only practicing the form of meditation which you have initially selected for yourself. This helps you give your mind and body ample opportunity to get to know it. The growing security you will gain will open the door to deep meditation experiences.

After a while, you might notice that the current method does not appeal to you after all. It goes without saying that you can then change the method if you decide that it doesn't suit you. However, I would advise that if you decide on one form, you should be committed to giving it a real chance.

Success cannot be instant. As a general rule of thumb, I recommend staying with a method for at least three months of daily meditation.

Perhaps you have been practicing one form for a while and are very familiar with it, and now you are ready to try something new and are curious about change. In this case, nothing is stopping you from trying the next form of meditation! You can always go back to the previous meditation if the new form doesn't suit you.

Introduction to various forms of meditation

In this section, I would like to introduce a few forms of meditation so you can gain an impression of the range of different meditations available and find the one which best suits your tastes. These descriptions are all based on my personal experience which may derive and may vary from the traditional methods. I do not just want to repeat traditional instructions that you may find in other sources but to emphasize those aspects that have been most useful to me to have a successful meditation experience. Feel free to find your own way of practicing them.

Dynamic Meditation

Characteristics: Active, focused on body and emotions.

Meditation tradition: My explanation is based on a meditation which was created by Osho, who was known under different names throughout his life. He was a spiritual teacher who had created different meditation forms for his followers; this one is one of his most famous. He died in 1990 in Poona, India.

If you are planning the dynamic meditation, I recommend selecting a location where you are able to make quite a bit of noise.

The dynamic meditation is split into four phases of 15 minutes each. It is a physically demanding meditation as it starts with a quarter of an hour of jumping. To do this, stand with your feet shoulder width apart, your knees bent slightly and your arms pointing up in the air. Then hop into the air. You make the hopping movement by pushing the knees out to straight each time and then letting out a "Hu!" with every landing. On breathing out, the arms are bent at your sides, similar to the chicken dance. You don't have to hop very high, in fact it's enough if only your heels leave the floor. Feel the movement, feel your breath, feel your weight which is being carried by the ground.

After quarter of an hour, this first phase should end abruptly with you freezing in the position you ended the hopping phase in. Try and hold the position as best you can. My arms always felt quite heavy after a while so I gradually let them sink to my sides in line with how I felt. In this phase, feel the rigidity after the fluid movement of the first phase. Feel the peace after the activity. Feel your breath and your heartbeat. Focus your attention inwards and on what is happening in your body and in your feelings.

This is then followed by an emotional phase. Now you can spend 15 minutes letting out all the feelings which you currently perceive: laughing, crying, shouting (a cushion is a very good way of damping the noise) and so on. Allow your body to follow these emotions. You can sit down or lie down. You can roll around on the floor or curl up in the corner. You can make all the noises which go along with this. Simply let go!

The last phase is the rest phase. In this phase you can lie comfortably on the floor and rest. The emotions can calm down, as can the breathing and the mind. Feel your weight on the floor, your breathing and the thoughts in your head. Here, peace is able to spread within you. This peace fills your entire head and then your body. It completely relaxes you.

You can find a lot of information about this meditation online or in books. Deuter also offers a special CD with musical accompaniment to the four phases (see "Useful Resources"). This has the advantage that you don't have to look at the clock to realize when it is time to change phases.

The first time I tried this meditation, I did it in a group and swore never to do it again! It was tiring, both mentally and physically, but especially emotionally. Nevertheless, it moved something inside of me because after a while I felt the urge to do it again. I decided to give it another try. This time it wasn't in the group, but on my own at home. Yes, it was still tiring, but I also benefited greatly from it. It had a purifying effect—first the physical exertion, then releasing the pent-up emotions. Over a period of several weeks, I did the meditation daily and it left me feeling strengthened and liberated.

If you decide to do this form of meditation, I recommend informing the people around you of your plans. After all, this meditation may lead to you making loud emotional noises, which may confuse other people. Assure everyone that everything they hear in the next hour is part of the meditation.

Whirling

Characteristics: Active, physically challenging, centering.

Meditation tradition: I got to know this meditation as
a version of Osho's meditation. But whirling is also
originated among Sufis, the practitioners of Sufism, where
this meditation is part of their religious tradition.

To start with, I would like to emphasize that this meditation is not suitable for you if you have difficulties with physical coordination.

You should also take some precautions when preparing for whirling. First, you need some free space around you. Clear any chairs, tables and sharp objects out of the way. If you own a non-slip gymnastics mat, roll it out on the floor in the middle of your space. It is also possible that you might feel sick during the meditation, so it is also a good idea to have a bucket nearby (neither I nor anyone else I know has ever needed a bucket, but it is better to be safe than sorry!).

When it comes to clothing, I always prefer to do this meditation barefoot. I would advise against slippy socks as these could cause you to fall.

Start by standing in a relaxed position in the middle of the room with your arms hanging loosely by your sides. Then slowly start to turn your body on its own axis and increase the tempo to as fast as feels right for you. It doesn't matter whether you turn left or right; find out which direction works best for you.

Try not to focus your eyes, but instead stare straight ahead and allow your view to roll over everything that is turning, leaving your environment blurred. You can control the tempo either with your feet or by how high you lift your arms. The first time you do this, try out some different positions and you will soon feel the effects.

It's quite normal for you to get dizzy and to move around the room somewhat. That is why you made room for yourself beforehand! The mat under your feet can help you to remain approximately in the middle of the space and you can therefore feel through your feet where the "safe zone" is. Simply move back into the center of the room every time you go off on a tangent.

Whatever you do, don't attempt to stop spinning to look where you are or where you have to be, it won't work. Simply move back to your starting point by spinning.

As a help to stop you from tumbling over, imagine you are a screw that is being screwed deeper and deeper into the floor.

If you feel sick—and I always feel a little sick during this meditation—remember not to focus your vision and limit your tempo if required.

This all sounds rather difficult, unpleasant and tiring, but it is in fact quite the opposite. If you concentrate on spinning and don't focus your vision, this can cause a change in your perception to such an extent that it almost seems as if you are standing still. This is quite a cool feeling! The room around you can spin and move as it wants to, but you are standing still and are centered in yourself. What a wonderful analogy for everyday life, don't you think?!

According to the whirling instructions, the spinning phase should be 45 minutes long. However, this doesn't strictly have to be the case. When I did the meditation for the first time, I was only able to do the exercise for 15 to 20 minutes before I had had enough.

So whenever you feel like you've had enough or if you already did 45 minutes, make a decision to carefully let yourself fall to the ground. Simply allow yourself to slump carefully, taking care not to hurt yourself.

As you are now probably very dizzy, the best thing to do is to take up the following position: while kneeling, tip your body forwards, place your arms in front of you and your forehead on the floor. Calmly breathe in and out.

This rest phase should last for at least 15 minutes. When the dizziness has subsided, I always let myself fall to the side and then I lie down comfortably.

Feel what's happening within yourself—the inner and exterior movement, the body, the thoughts, the inner and external silence of the body and the mind.

Deuter also offers music for this meditation which accompanies the session.

It is obviously not possible to make notes during this meditation. You have to wait until the rest phase to do this.

Walking Meditation

Characteristics: Genuinely active, good against the monkey mind.

Meditation tradition: In the West, walking meditation is primarily known in connection with the Buddhist monk Thich Nhat Hanh, who practices it in a less rigid way than the traditional Zen Buddhism instructs, where for example the position of the hands is prescribed.

Walking meditation is a very purist, simple-to-practice form of meditation. It can be done both inside and outside. Outside you have somewhat more space; however, it is sometimes easier to keep your concentration inside, especially when you start meditating. Select the environment in which you feel most at ease.

It is up to you whether you do this in shoes, socks or barefoot. It can feel fantastic to do this barefoot on grass in summer.

If you practice the walking meditation inside, you can walk back and forth or in small circles. Outside you have more space, so look for a pleasant place. This doesn't have to be somewhere natural; I've even done a walking meditation on the streets of Manhattan before.

There isn't much to say about this meditation. As the name suggests, it's all about walking. Therefore, walk. Walk slowly. Walk attentively. Walk consciously. Walk in a concentrated manner.

Feel your feet as they touch the floor and then lift up and leave it again. Feel the change in your weight distribution.

Feel your hips as they move with every step. Feel your upper body and how it adjusts to the walking movements.

Feel your breathing, which you can adjust to the rhythm of your steps.

Your vision is relaxed on the floor one or two meters in front of you, with your neck and arms relaxed.

It is not about arriving at a destination with your walking. It is not a journey from A to B. The walking merely offers a vehicle to come into contact with yourself.

With every conscious step you take, you take a step further into yourself. With every movement which you consciously perceive, you become more conscious of yourself.

You can focus your mind very easily on the movement, changes, weight distribution and breathing. This allows you to closely integrate your mind into the activity—the perfect prerequisite for meditation experiences. Go for it!

Nadabrahma Meditation

Characteristics: Active sitting, humming, emotionally warming.

Meditation tradition: I learned this meditation as an adapted
version by Osho. Originally it is based on an ancient
Tibetan technique, that concentrates on humming.

The Nadabrahma meditation starts with a half-hour phase in which you simply sit in a relaxing position and hum. In other words, you allow your body to hum. You allow any sound to emerge from your mouth which wants to come out. The sounds which feel right.

This is a liberating, releasing, non-articulated mode of communication with yourself and your environment. Here you can get closer to yourself, your inner self, which expresses itself through humming.

The vibrations created by the humming also relax your body. Your breathing, diaphragm and inner organs are soothed and softly massaged.

This is followed by two 7 minute phases of gentle arm movements. The basic posture stays the same—you remain in a relaxed sitting position.

In the first phase, you move your arms as if you were doing the breaststroke. First, you hold your hands next to one another in front of your chest with the palms facing up. Then you extend your arms out as far as you can and make an arc to the left and the right outwards to your sides and then back to your chest.

The most important thing about these movements is that you make them as slow as possible, almost as if you were not moving at all. If your upper body would like to move somewhat as part of the arm movement, allow it to.

The mental approach to this movement is as follows: you can give everything that you are and that you have in the world without losing anything. Give the gift of your uniqueness to the world, show yourself and your individuality. You are a gift to the world as you are. And you remain yourself, in yourself, as the center of the movement, the center of everything that you are.

As soon as the first 7 minutes are up, your arms should remain in exactly the position they are, and then the next phase begins.

To transition into this phase, rotate your palms downwards slowly from the position you are in and begin to do the same arm movement in the opposite direction. The arms trace an arc from the outside to the front, until the arms are straight out in front of you and then pulled in towards the chest, from where they begin to move to the outside again.

The emotional approach is now as follows: you can take everything that the world has to offer without taking anything away from anyone. Everything that you need and want, everything that you are missing, everything you desire is available to you.

In my experience, everyone finds one of the two mental activities more difficult than the other, either giving or receiving. Observe yourself closely. Which are you better at? How does this change over the weeks?

In the final phase, which lasts 15 minutes, allow peace to descend over you. You leave the humming and arm movements behind, gradually winding these down. You can stay sitting or lying down, as you wish.

Use this phase to feel what effect the humming, giving and taking had on you. What changed? Was anything opened up or released? How do you feel now?

Your breathing is calm, your voice is serene, your body is peaceful, you give and take in balance, you are in your center.

Vipassana Meditation

Characteristics: Peaceful, trains body perception.

Meditation tradition: Vipassana is based on ancient Buddhism
traditions. I learned to know it as "one of the world's
most ancient techniques of meditation." It is taught in
different forms, some active some inactive, so don't
be astonished to find different descriptions of it.

There are many very long and detailed instructions available for
Vipassana meditation. Here, I would like to avoid excessive details
and just communicate the essentials for meditation beginners.

Adopt a relaxed posture—the recommended positions
are sitting or lying down. Breathe in and then out. Focus your
attention on your breathing.

Perhaps you can perceive your breathing in your nose, perhaps
in your lungs or in your belly, it doesn't matter where.

Direct your attention completely to the movement of your
breathing. Allow the words "in" and "out" to form in rhythm with
your breathing.

When you have the feeling that you have clearly focused your
attention and have switched off from everyday life, then extend
your focus to your entire body. Feel where things are happening
and follow the first impulse of your physical feelings.

Perhaps it is a sound which shifts into focus in your attention.
Or perhaps it is a visual image, a picture in your mind's eye. It
might be something uncomfortable on your body. It can also be a
mood or feeling. Whatever it is, give it your full attention.

Follow how your feeling changes as soon as you have given it
your full focus. You can describe it to yourself with words, images
or simply perceive it. Then follow this changing feeling with all
your attention. It is possible that the feeling will fade into the
background after a while or will disappear completely. If this is
the case, observe yourself again afresh and direct your attention
to the next impulse you feel in your body.

Keep your attention focused. This attention is not some
penetrating curiosity, but peaceful concentration with the wish

of looking at yourself and what is happening within you in detail. Every feeling starts afresh in every moment. Every bodily sensation is different than the one before it if you only observe closely enough.

Follow, direct and observe your attention for the duration of an hour or the amount of time you have defined.

Mantra Meditation

Characteristics: Peaceful, calming through repetition.

Meditation tradition: Mantras are originated in the Vedic
tradition of India. This technique is an essential part
of the Hindu tradition and practiced within Buddhism
and other religions. But also the repeated prayers
with a rosary in Catholicism are a variation of it.

Mantras are words or sentences which are repeated in rhythm
with breathing.

There are of course numerous words or sentences which you
can use as a mantra. In religious traditions, a mantra is usually given
from the master to the pupil. However, this is not necessary in
your case. By the same token, it doesn't have to be a meaningful
mantra from a foreign language, such as Sanskrit.

When it comes to selecting the right mantra, I believe that
you can take any word which appeals to you. A lot of people use
words such as love, peace or quiet. But as Aspies, many of us
have words which we like a lot, which sound nice or which trigger
pleasant feelings or other positive sensations. You are completely
free to select one of these words as your mantra.

Many mantras which consist of sentences are said in melodies
communicated over generations.

You can of course use these melodies or you can create your
own. The most well-known mantra of this type is the Gayatri
mantra in Sanskrit. I once read the translation of the words, but
they didn't mean much to me. As I said, this is not necessary. I
find that it calms me down to sing the words, irrespective of what
they mean.

When meditating with a mantra, it doesn't matter what
posture you take up. You can be walking, sitting, standing or lying
down—whatever you like.

You can say your mantra out loud or speak it within yourself.
Simply follow the rhythm of your breath. If you take a short word,
for example, you can say the mantra every time you breathe
out and then breathe in in silence, perceiving your breathing in

between mantras. Or you can distribute the mantra and syllables over the process of breathing in and out. Alternatively, you can also say it in the pause between breaths. Try experimenting to find out what feels most natural to you.

Repeat your mantra for an hour or for the period you defined. It is possible that over time the meaning of the word is lost, and it breaks down into individual components, syllables, sounds and emotions.

It is possible that the melody changes and dances, that the volume varies or disappears completely. You don't have to force this or guide this, simply let it happen. Observe, repeat, feel and return to your inner self.

Silent Sitting

Characteristics: Peaceful, purist, mentally challenging.

Meditation tradition: Meditating in silent sitting is called Zazen in the Zen tradition, but it is also known as contemplation in Christian traditions. Different religions give different instructions. The Zen tradition for example has rules governing the sitting itself—rules of entering the room, beating the cushion, the correct posture and even how to walk.

I'm describing an interpretation of silent sitting without strict rules. However, if you enjoy attention to detail, fixed sequences and rituals, then the rules integrated in Zazen could have a calming influence on you. The good thing is that even at Zazen groups, there is little interaction with others and that suits us Aspies very well.

Now let's talk about sitting. As preparation for the meditation, ensure you have a suitable place to sit (see Chapter 7, section on "General information on sitting meditation") and look for a suitable location (see Chapter 7, section on "Where should I meditate?"). My favorite place is in front of a white wall. This offers the advantage that there are very few visual stimuli in front of me, as I keep my eyes open slightly during meditation. You can of course also close your eyes, as you may find this easier to start with.

Now you simply sit until the time has expired; that is the secret. You decide with your decision, dedication, mindfulness and attention to make a meditation out of the act of sitting.

I could go into more detail about the inner contact, the perception of the body, mind and the wall, but all of these details would be my words, and these are things you should discover for yourself. I do not wish to direct and limit your meditation with my words.

So my advice is to just sit and meditate.

For more on this, please read the section in Chapter 9 on "When your mind is too loud." Having a piece of paper and meditation book to hand is also effective here (see Chapter 8 "Aids for Meditation").

Koan Meditation

Characteristics: Peaceful, mind-oriented.

Meditation tradition: Koans were developed during the Tang-Dynasty (Schlütter 2008), and are used by the Zen-practice. Today there are different famous Koan collections available, like The Blue Cliff Record.

Koans can be an excellent introduction to meditation for mind-oriented people and/or people who like to take things literally and imagine things visually.

Koans are short episodes which at first glance seem paradoxical and senseless. Here are a couple of examples as I remember them from hearsay:

> What does it sound like if a hand slaps itself?
> If a tree falls in the forest and nobody hears it, does it make a sound?
> The wave and the ocean are one.

Koans can also be short stories such as this:

> Two monks were watching a flag flapping in the wind. One said to the other, "The flag is moving."
> The other replied, "The wind is moving."
> Huineng overheard this. He said, "Not the flag, not the wind; mind is moving." (Wumen Hui-K'ai, *The Gateless Gate*, Yamada 2004, case 29, p.143)

For me as an Aspie, life is full of paradoxes, which is why this approach seems familiar. Koans can often be explained through rational thought, but that is not the purpose! The approach I teach is that the inconsistency which is at the basis of all things is revealed in the Koan and the aim is to feel this dissonance. You cannot find the essence of a Koan with rationality. You have to transfer the paradox, inconsistency and rationality into your own feelings to gain insight.

If you like this approach, I advise purchasing a Koan collection (see "Useful Resources") and selecting a Koan either randomly or by preference. Learn it by heart, hold it in your mind and consider it during meditation, either walking, sitting or lying down.

For an hour, break down the Koan with your mind, feel it in your body and in your emotions. Perhaps you will find a solution. Perhaps you will find a feeling. Perhaps you will find an insight.

Stay with one Koan. Even if you think that you've cracked it, believe me, there is much more within it to discover. Only change the Koan with caution.

Painting Mandalas

Characteristics: Peaceful, visually creative.

Meditation tradition: Mandalas have their origin in Buddhist and Hindu traditions, where they are often used for sacred art. In Christian religion the equivalent can be found for example in churches' rose windows. (Not to be confused with the active meditation from Osho called "mandala meditation.")

Many of us Aspies are visually oriented and are very receptive to symmetries, patterns, shapes and colors in all their details. That is why I would like to talk about mandalas here. Mandalas are graphical, geometric patterns, often circular in shape. The tradition of these patterns is very old, but nowadays they are also available in purpose-designed books (see "Useful Resources"). Painting these templates can be used as a meditation. This is a very creative form of meditation and one which is somewhat different to the other meditations described here.

When you paint mandalas, everything is up to you, from the templates to the colors.

First, look for a mandala template which appeals to you. There are some very detailed patterns which require lots of attention to detail when painting. There are also very purist, minimalist patterns which call for colors in large segments. Many templates are said to have certain energies or topics. You shouldn't let yourself be influenced by this. My tip: decide according to your mood and feeling. You can find templates in special mandala painting books or online. You can trace one from a book or create your own.

Next, select the tool of your choice, colored or felt tip pens, ink or paint.

As soon as you have decided on one material, select the colors which appeal to you. Perhaps you already have a vision in your mind of how the completed mandala should look. You could also simply start painting and allow it to flow from part to part.

Now everything is ready. Before you start painting, look for a place where you feel good and you will not be disturbed. This is no different to other meditations in terms of location; the only constraint is that you require sufficient lighting.

Painting mandalas is not just about painting and coloring, it is about the concentrated perception of shape and patterns. The shapes and colors are internalized during meditation, breathed in, becoming a mirror of your inner self.

Feel what the pattern does with you. Which emotions does it awaken? How does it feel when you trace the shape with your eyes and work on it with your hands?

The mandala serves as a means of access to contacting your inner self. Your time spent painting is the path which leads from the entrance.

Another very challenging variation of working with mandalas is to color the pattern with colored sand. This first requires the necessary sand, which you can get hold of at any DIY store, and second a very skilled sleight of hand.

The result cannot be preserved and that would also not be the purpose of the exercise. It is about the presence and the moments which you feel during its creation. "The path to the goal" so to speak. You can then allow the elements to take the sand away.

One thing applies to both the sand and painting technique—this is not about perfectionism. I know that this is not easy for a lot of us, but that is also part of the exercise. It doesn't all have to be perfect. Having the "courage to be average" is what my therapist called it. The artistic design here is a vehicle for meditation. Nobody is assessing your image. It is all about the experience you have during the painting.

I look forward to receiving the photos of your mandalas!

Have you read through all the meditation forms? Isn't it amazing that meditation can have so many different forms? Just as life itself. And you will even make it more differentiated, with your own personality.

When you felt particularly connected to one of the above forms, you are ready to read on and prepare your first meditation experience.

If you felt connected to more than one, make your choice wisely or just pick one at random, because you are always free to change the form later on. There is enough time to try all of them if you like!

If none of those descriptions made you curious to give it a try, I recommend picking one at random and going through the preparations. Maybe the preparation will clarify your needs and you can reconsider your choice. If not, just start; one method is as good as the other to achieve a fulfilling meditation experience.

Chapter 7

When, Where and What to Wear?

When should I meditate?

Now that you have likely decided to meditate every day, the only question remaining is what time is best to do so.

According to some ascetic approaches to meditation, specific meditations have to be practiced at certain times of the day (often incredibly early in the morning), or at least should be if they are to be effective. I do not believe that this is true. In my experience, the hour of day does not have a great impact on the effectiveness of meditation. After all, everyone has their own individual daily rhythm, the personal inner clock by which they tick. It is much more crucial to orient yourself according to these personal phases and to your general circumstances, such as working hours, family obligations, mealtimes and training times.

The first steps you take in meditation are facilitated by meditating at the same time every day. Your subconscious then gets used to this process and expects inward thoughts at this time of day, which makes switching off at this time easier and easier. Furthermore us Aspies mostly love our routine; as you see meditation loves routine too. I know myself that changing a reliable routine can be very unsettling and hence we try to avoid it. But life sometimes is just unpredictable and changes in the timetable have to be made. So it may not always be possible to meditate every day at the same time. If this is the case, try to meditate on as many days as possible and arrange the other days as best you can. In exceptional cases, for instance on very busy days, it is a better to just do 15 minutes meditation than to do none at all. The good news is that the more experience you gain with meditating the easier it will become to change your routine when required. You will learn how to deal with instability from the outside, because you find stability inside yourself.

Select the time which best suits your daily schedule. You should also take into account the things happening around you: if you would like to meditate at home, please take into account your family schedule. If you want to meditate in the afternoon at 3 o'clock but this is exactly the time when your children like to play, then it is very likely to make your meditation difficult. Perhaps you can select a time when you are home alone or a time when you will be undisturbed.

If you want to meditate outdoors, take the daylight hours into account, the temperatures and any possible distracting noises, such as traffic at rush hour.

If you would like to make it easy for yourself to begin with, it is best to select a time which you do not "squeeze" between stressful activities. Time constraints will make it more difficult to find the peace to meditate. However, if you can look back at positive meditation experiences over time, meditation between stressful activities can also have a balancing and calming effect.

Select the time which best suits your body's rhythm. If you are someone who finds it hard to wake up in the morning and has problems getting into gear, then it is likely to be difficult in the long term to keep to morning meditation times. By the same token, if you meditate when you are really tired, there is a greater danger that you will fall asleep during passive meditation and this also makes the practice unnecessarily difficult. As an alternative, you can use an active morning meditation to start the day with some energy. In contrast, I find that active meditation before bed can make falling asleep difficult.

When you decide on the right time for you, set up your place of meditation so that it is ready when your meditation time comes round.

Early in the morning it may still be very cold so ensure that it is warm enough for you to sit comfortably. Perhaps your favorite show is on TV in the afternoon, so ensure you have set your video recorder. If you select a time around sunset, then remember to turn on a light when you start the meditation unless you want to end your meditation sitting in the dark.

If you're not home alone during a meditation time, inform everyone else about your meditation and help them get used to leaving you undisturbed during this time.

No matter the time period which you choose, ensure that you consciously decide that the meditation time is time for you. Time that you give to yourself. Use it. Enjoy it!

Where should I meditate?

You don't need a monastery, a lotus pond or a Zen garden to meditate. You don't need a special place, nor even a separate room or a special corner if you don't want to use one or can't. Why? Because essentially you can meditate anywhere and everywhere, the main factor is that you feel comfortable there. The only prerequisite is that the place you select is suitable in terms of its space and noise level.

Meditating at home

The most well-known example of a meditation space is simply your room or somewhere at home. This is a familiar environment which exudes security. By the same token, you also have the freedom to set up an area specifically for this purpose. There, you can practice every form of meditation without having to worry about any undesired attention.

Your place of meditation could be a quiet corner in a room or a pleasant place at a window, perhaps even on your bed. It goes without saying that your place of meditation does not have to be your room, it could just as well be a soft rug in the bathroom or in the sanctuary of your cupboard.

Feel free to follow your personal needs in terms of sensory issues. Choose a place that takes into account your individual likes and dislikes when it comes to the brightness of light, different smells or ambient noises. Meditation time is wellness time so take care that you feel well where you meditate.

The only recommendation I have about meditating at home, which I cannot reiterate enough, is to inform anyone else living with you that you do not want to be disturbed.

Meditating outside the home

There are numerous other closed spaces outside the home where you might feel comfortable to meditate: in the quiet peace of the library, in a church (you don't have to be a believer to enjoy the atmosphere), in the grand surroundings of a museum or in the anonymous liveliness of the subway.

If you decide on a public location, I do not recommend practicing active, attention-grabbing meditations. You also have to be prepared for disturbance by other visitors to this location.

Or you can practice meditation outside. Many Aspies have special places in nature which serve as their place of retreat, allowing them to escape interaction with people for a while. Are you one of these Aspies? If so, then try meditating in the park, the forests, next to the river, in the freedom of an open field, in your garden, at the foot of a tree, next to a pond, at the seaside—whichever you are lucky enough to live near. You can even immerse yourself in the anonymous buzz of the city.

In public locations outdoors, such as the park or forest, active meditations are also possible as long as you are not disturbed by the possibility of being watched.

For more on this, please read the section later in this chapter on "General information on meditating in nature."

As you can see, there are many ways of finding a good location for meditation. In your own interests, select a place where you simply feel good.

How long should I meditate for?

There is a much quoted Zen statement on this: "If you don't have half an hour to spare every day to meditate, then meditate for an hour." In other words, if you don't have half an hour to spare every day, then you are particularly in need of creating breaks in your schedule. I highly recommend that beginners attempt to meditate every day for between 30 and 60 minutes.

In my experience, as a beginner you need at least 15 minutes to switch off your mind from everyday life and shift it towards meditation. To ensure that you also enjoy the benefits of the meditation, I therefore recommend 30 minutes as a minimum. This is a recommendation, not a must. If it is not possible for you—because of your life circumstances or simply your preference—then don't use this as an excuse not to even begin. I've often heard excuses like this: "I'd love to meditate but I don't have an hour free every day, so it's not really an option for me." That's a comfortable excuse. It is the same principle as 15 minutes exercise every day still being more beneficial than no exercise at all.

If you're serious about meditation, then you don't *have* to do it every day, you *want* to do it every day. Allow yourself a couple of weeks for the first successes to arrive. Over the course of the year, you will find it increasingly easy to enter meditation, allowing you to reduce the time and nevertheless benefit by the same amount.

During my years in meditation groups, I often detected some sort of hidden competition to see who had meditated for the longest. This led to statements such as: "I meditate for three hours every day." And I asked myself: "And? Are you a better person now?" If you feel it does you good, then do it. But meditation is about the quality, not the quantity of the experience. It's better to do half an hour concentrated meditation than to sit around for three hours just for the sake of meditating for three hours.

As a beginner, quality can only be attained through quantity. Just like learning other things, such as a musical instrument, it is all about practice. And if you can't practice, there will be no end result. That is why I recommend 30 to 60 minutes a day.

In the future, you will develop a feeling for the rhythm which does you good. In some phase of your life you may have the need for longer meditation, for instance when there are things in your life which are straining you. By the same token, during stable phases of your life, it may be that you feel that you can shorten your meditation times.

CDs with suitable music for active meditation generally run for one hour. However, if you only want to invest half an hour, then shorten all the phases proportionally. A 30 minute phase therefore becomes 15 minutes long.

If one day you don't have time to meditate during your selected time period, for example because someone comes to the door, a long awaited package arrives or a friend comes earlier than expected, then it's no problem to end the meditation prematurely. This freedom also applies to active meditation, which follows a pre-set sequence of phases. You are the master of your own meditation and can therefore decide when it is over. Essentially, meditation can be ended at any moment. When you are completely within the meditation with your attention, then you can end it at any time, it doesn't need a specific start or finish.

And what should I wear?

This question is simple and easy to answer, because my number one rule is this: make sure it is comfortable!

Many Aspies have preferences when it comes to certain materials and fabrics. From that point of view, you can go with your personal wishes on this one and wear your favorite clothes if that's what you want—you can even meditate in the nude at home but make sure the curtains are closed!

For active meditation, you should ensure that you can move freely in the clothes you're wearing. For passive meditation, it is important that you can sit or lie comfortably in your clothing of choice. You shouldn't wear anything too tight or rigid which could cut off your circulation.

If you're meditating outside, consider wearing clothes which suit the climatic conditions, ensuring that you are equipped to deal with wind, adverse weather and sunshine.

Special clothing for meditation is also available, such as meditation scarves. However, these do not have any deeper meaning other than being a nice accessory.

If you want to use specific clothing for your meditation, you can make putting these clothes on into a key part of your meditation ritual.

General information on sitting meditation
What should I sit on?

The most obvious question when it comes to sitting meditation is: on what? There are numerous different options for meditating while sitting. All that sets meditation chairs apart is that they are made for sitting on the floor.

Here, I would like to briefly outline the various forms of meditation chairs available (see also "Useful Resources").

MEDITATION CUSHION

The most popular option is the meditation cushion. The basic posture is sitting on the cushion with your legs tucked underneath you so that your shinbone and the top of your foot are touching the floor.

These cushions are available with various fillings, some softer, some harder, some made of cotton and some with types of grain. The cut of the cushion determines the height at which you sit, although this is also influenced by how hard it is and how much filling is inside the cushion. In general, beginners tend to find high cushions more comfortable.

MEDITATION BENCH

Meditation benches are generally made of wood. In contrast to meditation cushions, you're able to tuck your legs under the bench.

They are available both with straight and curved legs, which ensure that your back stays straight. There are also versions with small cushions integrated, tiny rests or folding foot components which allow the bench to be easily stored or transported.

One elegant version of the meditation bench is the *benchbow*, which is inspired by the round shape of a bow.

FLOOR CHAIRS

So-called floor chairs are also very comfortable. They consist of a metal frame in the form of a slanting letter "L" which is covered in material. The front is padded with a cushion, allowing you to comfortably lean back against the upright back rest. You can have your legs either crossed or stretched out in front of you.

These chairs are also available in a folding version.

FLOOR SEATING

But you can go even lower! You can of course simply sit on the floor. In order to make this somewhat more comfortable, you can place a zabuton (a flat, wide pillow) underneath you, and this is also a recommended tip for making a meditation bench more comfortable. A cheaper option would simply be to place a woolen cover underneath you.

If this position on the floor is too uncomfortable for you, you are also quite entitled to sit on a normal chair. Or in an armchair, on the sofa or on a bed. The quality of your meditation will not suffer if you're not sitting on a special meditation chair. Your body should simply be able to sit comfortably.

How should I sit?

Most pictures of sitting meditation depict the meditating person in the lotus position or a similar yoga position— cross-legged. There are also concepts of meditation that state that you *have to* sit in this position so that the energy can flow correctly and that you can experience true meditation.

In my experience, you don't need to be able to sit in the lotus position. In fact, you don't even need to cross your legs. It doesn't matter how you sit. You can place your legs on something, bend them, stretch them out, whatever you like.

You can even move. As you would expect, this is something that is frowned upon in many other meditation books. It certainly doesn't give your meditation any added value if your legs go to sleep. I think we can leave that to the ascetics, unless you are looking to test your physical boundaries in your meditation, that is. For more on this, please read the section in Chapter 4 on "Meditation and body."

If it gets uncomfortable, most times you don't need to change your position a great deal. If you notice that you are uncomfortable and that your body is experiencing unpleasant tension, then remind yourself that your body is allowed to be comfortable. It might sound funny, but perhaps your body can be comfortable in this position if only you would allow it to be. If not, ask yourself which position would be necessary for your body to feel comfortable again. Start to adopt this position, carefully, attentively and gradually. Perhaps you don't have to change the position as much as you would have thought. Allow your feelings to guide you until you have found a comfortable position.

What else should I pay attention to?

No matter which piece of furniture you choose to place your posterior on, there are a couple of rules which apply across the board.

COMFORTABLE PADDING

So far in my life, I have spent several thousand hours meditating. Therefore take some advice from an experienced meditating body: it cannot be comfortable enough. After a certain amount of time even the softest meditation chair seems hard and uncomfortable. As a result, especially when you are new to meditation, it is a very good idea to have an extra pillow ready or be prepared to change your sitting situation completely during the meditation.

COMFORTABLE CLOTHING
Please pay attention to ensure that your clothing is comfortable, even in a sitting position. Avoid constricting materials and hems. For more information on this, please read the section on what to wear earlier in this chapter.

Warmth
I've always been very sensitive to the cold. Many Aspies are not at all sensitive to this or do not pay attention to it. That is why I am reminding you here always to remember that your body can cool off when sitting in the same position for a long time. You can take this into consideration from the start and wrap up warm. In addition, you could place a blanket nearby in case you need some extra heat. I also like having a hot water bottle on hand to keep my feet or kidneys warm.

View
Most people, especially when they start out with meditation, like to meditate in sitting with their eyes closed. This already excludes a source of external stimuli and allows the attention to be directed inwards more easily.

Meditating with your eyes open requires some practice. If you would like to meditate with open eyes, the view from where you are sitting is very important, even if your vision is unfocused and looking downwards. Whether it's a white wall, a mirror, a window, a mandala or something else, it is your responsibility to select something which promotes your meditation.

For more on this please look again at the sections on "When should I meditate?", "Where should I meditate?" and "And what should I wear?"

General information on active meditation

By my definition, active meditation is meditation carried out with movement. Active meditations can take many different forms. Some involve jumping and dancing, while others mean sitting and moving your arms slowly. However, there are several factors which play a role in all active meditations and I would like to list these here.

Health

Some active meditations can be truly challenging physically. Your health has top priority. You are responsible for your own well-being and your health, and that also goes for during meditation. That is why I am always aware of my body and the feedback it is giving me. Something which might be fine for you and your body on one day, might be too strenuous on another day.

You can adjust meditation practice so that it fits your requirements. For instance, you can make small movements out of large ones, slow movements out of quick ones.

One aspect of health is bodily hygiene, which is a must for us as Aspies and which has to be as thoroughly planned as all other everyday tasks. Therefore, after meditation which has left you sweating, a shower and a change of clothes is ideal. You should therefore plan this time into your meditation routine.

Space

Movements need space. When selecting the ideal location for an active meditation, it is therefore important to ensure that you have sufficient space for the required movement, ideally considerably more. Also consider that in your eagerness to meditate, you may possibly not be able to move as precisely as you normally would. It is therefore advisable to plan somewhat more space, as a safety zone so to speak. The area you choose should be free of any objects which could lead to injury if you deviate from the planned movements. You should also ensure that nothing valuable can be broken, such as vases, porcelain figurines or model airplanes.

Clothing

During active meditation, the body may warm up, similar to a sports workout. Just like during sports, it is important to wear clothes in which you can move as freely as possible.

Many active meditations consist of various phases. Each phase is linked with a different type of activity. They generally begin with a lot of movement and end in the final phase with a relaxing posture, sitting or lying down. This places various demands on your clothing, which shouldn't be either too hot or too airy. Therefore, I recommend going for the "onion look" (yes, I also always imagine it literally, although it doesn't sound very tasty to wear a raw onion!). In other words, wear several layers of thin clothing, allowing yourself to add or shed garments as required.

Consideration

Some Aspies find it difficult to relate to the requirements of other people, which can result in them being perceived more impolitely than intended. That is why I would like to talk about consideration here. Active meditation can result in you making a lot of noise on occasions. If not through the movements and expression of feelings themselves, then perhaps through the background music which supports active meditation in its various phases.

Ask the people around you if the meditation disturbs them and, if so, look for mutual solutions which suit both sides. Meditating at a different time or turning down the volume of your stereo might be a good start. If you are too loud when you let out your emotions, you can use a pillow to great effect to dampen the noise.

Consideration is of course also reciprocal, so from your point of view you can also expect consideration that you will go undisturbed during meditation. Discuss this ahead of your meditation with the people around you.

For more on this please re-read the sections on "When should I meditate?", "Where should I meditate?" and "And what should I wear?"

General information on meditating in nature

Nature has a calming effect on the souls of people. In general, the color green has a calming influence. It was no coincidence that for years Windows had the image of a green hill with a blue sky above it as the default desktop background picture.

Nature often offers Aspies a place of retreat, some time out from society and communication, and of course some healthy fresh air. For most of us, nature is a place of freedom because we always spend so much time in enclosed spaces such as at school, in our job and at home. An excursion into nature is therefore symbolic of a timeout. The peace and imposing gentle beauty of nature are true sources of energy. As a result of all these positive characteristics, nature is an ideal place to meditate, allowing you to feel comfortable.

How does it work?

What form does meditation take in a natural setting? First, you can of course use nature as a place to practice your selected meditation, whether it be active or passive. Nature therefore becomes your meditation room outdoors; however, your meditation method does not have to be any different to the one you would practice indoors. Outdoors, you need not worry about a lack of space for active meditation.

Moreover, you can also use nature itself as the meditation object. The natural sounds, smells, sensations and images offer incomparable access to meditation. Watch how the leaves and grasses sway, the water flows, listen to the rustling of the leaves or the lapping of the water, follow the movement of the clouds, open yourself up to the details around you or the imposing backdrop of an entire landscape.

At this point, I would like to repeat once more that you are the only one who can make this natural experience into a meditation through your inner mindset. Open yourself up to the beauty of your surroundings and to the honesty of nature. Open yourself to your inner self, with honesty and without any artificial barriers. You are part of nature. You are a living being. You are life.

What should I pay attention to?
TIME OF DAY
In nature, you are dependent on natural light conditions. Therefore, please note that the daylight hours change during the year and that you may have to adapt your meditation time accordingly.

SPECTATORS
If you don't have your own large piece of land where you can meditate, you may have to deal with possible spectators during a meditation in nature. You should therefore consider in advance whether you can cope with this. Sometimes I have experienced being looked at slightly inquisitively but no more than that.

A friend of mine lives in a heavily wooded area where she would go on a daily basis to practice her walking meditation. In her village, it was normal for people to greet each other when out and about, and perhaps exchange a few words. However, as she did not want to be disturbed during her meditation, my friend had a T-shirt printed which stated in large letters: I am meditating, please do not disturb! And that says it all. From that point on, she was only greeted with smiling but silent faces on her meditation route.

CLOTHING

When meditating in nature, wearing appropriate clothing is a matter of common sense. You should adjust your clothing to suit the climatic conditions and the weather, protecting yourself against rain, cold or sunshine. If you are susceptible to bladder infections, as many women are, you should be cautious about sitting outside in the cold for an hour. Insulating clothing or seating can help in this case.

HAIR

One tip which I would like to give to everyone with long hair is to tie your hair up when meditating outside, or wear a hairband or a hat. Personally, I find it extremely unpleasant to constantly have my hair flapping in my face. This can also impact your concentration.

ALTERNATIVES

If the weather does not allow you to meditate outside as usual, have some alternatives ready ahead of time so that you do not have to cancel your meditation due to the weather.

For more on this, please go back to the sections on "When should I meditate?", "Where should I meditate?" and "And what should I wear?"

Chapter 8

Aids for Meditation

In order to have a successful start into meditation there are several aids that might help you to get started. None of these aids is essential and you could do just as well without them—but some of them might give you support in your new experience of meditation. Have a look yourself at what might help you.

Alarm

When us Aspies concentrate on something, we can often forget time and space. Having a clock is therefore a very useful way of keeping an eye on the time during your meditation. An alarm clock is even more useful. If you set an alarm for the end of your meditation, you can completely let yourself go during your practice and forget everything around you.

I prefer an alarm with a soft ring tone so that I'm not abruptly shaken out of my meditation by a loud beeping noise. Using MP3 alarms or simply your mobile phone alarm, nowadays it is easy to select the right alarm sound for you.

There are also special meditation clocks available which are only different due to the fact that they run backwards, like a countdown. Meditation alarms are even available, which contain a chime which rings out softly when the time is up. Finally, there is even a CD available which remains completely silent until a gong sound hits at the end of the meditation period.

Music

Many people use music as an aid to meditation. You can do this if you would like to, although you certainly don't have to. Many people choose music because it has a calming effect and facilitates entry into the meditation. Many Aspies are however very sensitive to audible impulses. If it isn't too much for you, music can help you focus your hearing, drowning any possible background noise away.

If you're looking for suitable meditation music, then I would certainly suggest listening to a lot of different CDs before you decide which one is for you. Avoid just listening to the start of the CD, listen to various points in the disc as the music and volume often change over its duration.

The various types of meditation music available are listed below.

Instrumental

The most common meditation music is instrumental, which features calming melodies and perhaps natural sounds. There is an almost inexhaustible range of relaxation music on offer. Only your preference can decide what is right for you. As people's musical tastes vary so strongly, I would only like to give one CD recommendation for readers who perhaps need a starting point. A justified classic is *Angel Love* from Aeoliah.

Active meditations

CDs are available for the most popular active meditations, helping to acoustically separate and support the various phases of meditation.

Here, I can particularly recommend the music from Deuter (see "Useful Resources"). Although it is not completely to my taste, it does offer the advantage that it has a large range covering various meditations.

Mantras
Special CDs are also available for mantras. However, in general they are only suitable for the start of a meditation because the individual pieces are too short for longer meditations.

The CDs from Deva Premal are also highly recommended as they are beautiful to listen to and helpful in learning the melodies (see "Useful Resources").

Preferences
Although low-key music is generally thought of as meditation music, any type of music can be selected. As with everything else in meditation, it is completely down to your own personal tastes. You can use jazz, techno, metal, whatever! I've even meditated with clients to heavy metal before, because we both enjoy it. One surprising aspect of heavy metal is often very good lyrics, which can be nicely integrated into the meditation. You can also put together your own CD or MP3 music lists to accompany your practice.

Humming
One aspect of Asperger Syndrome can be a love of humming. I like to hum too, especially to relax me in stressful situations. You can of course integrate this into your meditation. In the Nadabrahma meditation it even forms a fixed component in the meditation sequence. Simply hum. If it does you good, then it's great.

Tuning fork

A different means of accessing meditation acoustically is offered by the tuning fork. I would recommend the Om tuner from Biosonics (see "Useful Resources"). The tuner has a very peaceful, deep tone, which directly relaxes my breathing and exudes peace.

Be creative

Perhaps you are relaxed by the ticking of a clock or a metronome. Perhaps the noise of traffic or the snoring of your dog. Surround yourself with the sounds which are conducive to your relaxation and concentration, whatever they may be. If you're musical, you can of course compose your own music for your meditation. In this respect, your artistic expression has no limits.

Earplugs

Many Aspies are highly sensitive to noise. Meditation helps make you more tolerant to acoustic stimuli over time, but until you have mastered this, meditation doesn't have to be a torture.

In order to direct your concentration inwards, it helps to reduce any outside stimuli. For your ears, you can use earplugs or noise-cancelling headphones.

Another option is to concentrate your hearing on the accompanying music, washing out other background noises and keeping them where they belong—in the background.

Writing material
Meditation book

In my opinion, writing in a meditation book is a very good idea. In a meditation book, you can record all your experiences in connection with your meditation practice and in this way maintain an overview of your development in the long term. To do this, many of my clients look for particularly attractive books, while some decorate the books with favorite photos or paintings. In these modern times, you can of course also do this on the PC. Whatever the case, the appearance of your meditation book is completely up to you. Sometimes, your meditation book also becomes a diary or a diary becomes a meditation book, when meditation practice becomes a real part of your life.

You can take the meditation book with you to your place of meditation and have a pen at hand. After completing the meditation, you can then record some notes.

As a starting point, you can think about the following questions:

- How did you feel during the meditation?
- How did your body feel?
- What thoughts went through your head?
- Did you have any ideas or insights during the meditation?
- What emotions were stirred up?
- How do you feel now?
- How does your body feel now?
- What thoughts are now at the forefront of your mind?

You don't necessarily have to formulate your thoughts into words, you can also simply paint colors which represent your feelings or give your current feelings grades like at school. A young person who I worked with was a great fan of cars and he expressed his feelings in his own scale of automobiles, from a VW Beetle right up to a Porsche.

Instead of only making notes after the meditation, you can also write ahead of the meditation how you're feeling and what is going through your head. This allows you to directly compare how the meditation may have changed your state of mind and feelings.

Paper for notes

Plain paper is also another excellent aid. It allows you to note down everyday things which go through your head during meditation and which you don't want to forget, such as "I have to buy more bread" or "remember to confirm that dental appointment." By writing these things down, you release them from your head and you can let these thoughts go without fear of forgetting them. This frees up your head for focusing on meditation.

Altar

Many people who meditate set up a small altar. The word "altar" is perhaps somewhat misleading, as this has religious connotations for many people. However, in this context it simply represents a place in the room which serves for reflection, thought and muse.

This can be a small table, a surface, a box, a shelf, a windowsill or a space on top of the sideboard. There, you can arrange pictures which you enjoy looking at, objects which calm you, flowers or a candle. This altar also becomes part of the meditation ritual when you sit down to meditate in front of it. As soon as you do this, your subconscious knows that peace will soon descend upon you.

You can also start and end active meditations with a minute of reflection in front of the altar, if you would like.

Even away from meditation, a glance at the altar can have a calming effect. When I was sitting on my bed in the evening in my old one-bedroom flat, I often enjoyed looking at the small table with a candle which served as my meditation altar. Simply glancing at this filled me with a sense of security, comfort and relaxation.

Meditation beads

Similar to the Rosary beads in the Catholic faith, meditation beads or arm bands are also available. These are pieces of string with beads or stones threaded onto them which can be touched or counted with the fingers during meditation.

Most of these have a certain number of beads usually relating to a particularly "holy number." I don't believe in concepts like that, but irrespective of how many beads are on the chain, it certainly helps to concentrate the mind.

Some books also suggest not counting the beads but only moving onto the next one if you find your thoughts wandering. This allows you to count at the end of the meditation how often you lost your concentration. I don't think much of this approach, which focuses on mistakes. Meditation is not about avoiding mistakes, but opening yourself to everything that comes, whether it be mistakes or truths. Do not focus on mistakes, focus on successes.

Candles

Candles or tea lights are common accessories for meditation. Sometimes they are also used as aids, allowing you to focus your concentration on one point—the flame of the candle.

Candles exude a peaceful, cozy atmosphere, provide warm, soft light and can therefore help put you in a relaxed mood.

However, due to the open fire, avoid using a candle for active meditations, as you may knock it over. For passive meditations, please always ensure that you have a safe candle stand.

Incense

Burning incense sticks during meditation is a very popular practice. Personally, I find that smoke smells disturb my concentration. Like me, many Aspies are sensitive to smells and this sensitivity can even be heightened during meditation due to the deep breathing involved. The smoke is only part of the ritual and has no influence on the quality of the meditation, which is why it is no problem to do without it.

However, if you like the idea of having a smell to support your meditation, try some different types of incense and always ensure that you have a safe stand for the smoldering stick.

Animals

As is the case for many Aspies, my pets give me very special type of support, and that's why I would like to address this topic here. I have a dog who rarely leaves my side because he loves snuggling up next to me, jumping on top of me and sleeping close by. My dog is calm and well-balanced, and his *joie de vivre* helps me to combat mood swings more effectively than any medicine ever could. He doesn't demand any complex interaction, doesn't have any hidden intentions, but instead shows directly what he wants. We also have two cats who love to snuggle up, but as is typical for cats they only look for physical contact when they are in the mood.

My pets are all very quiet and are therefore pleasant company for relaxing with.

In my study where I coach my clients, train bodywork and of course meditation, I also have my own place of meditation. There is a *zabuton*, which is a wide flat cushion, with a small meditation bench on top of it. This is placed in front of a white wall which I look at while I meditate. As soon as I sit down to meditate, one or two of my pets inevitably join me.

The dog tries to climb on top of me while one of the cats inevitably rubs up against my hips. Is this allowed during meditation? Of course it is. If it helps you relax, then of course it is allowed. If it distracts you and disrupts your concentration, then close the door so your pets cannot enter, or see it as a challenge and an exercise in concentration to meditate regardless of this distraction.

Watching animals is a relaxing activity in itself and can therefore be used as a stepping stone to starting a meditation. The vision of a dozing or snoring dog, whether quiet or somewhat louder, has a very calming effect. An aquarium can be just as calming, so it's no wonder that many screensavers depict this. The constant movement of ant farms, as are popular in the USA, can also be meditative. Simply follow your personal tastes and integrate this aspect of nature into your meditation.

Healthy diet

If you take time to read meditation books, sooner or later you will be confronted with the topic of diet. There are many approaches which teach that meditation is complemented by eating the correct diet. Vegetarianism is among the most well-known variations of these dietary concepts. I have tested a lot of these diets personally. I tried Ayurveda, vegetarianism, veganism, Zen monastery traditions and similar models. My verdict: diet does not have any direct influence on the practice of meditation. The correct diet for your body does however have an influence on your general well-being, and your well-being in turn influences your meditation. So use healthy common sense to pay attention to your diet.

I'm also unable to offer any opinions about coffee and alcohol in combination with meditation, as I don't drink the former and very seldom drink the latter, which does not put me in a good position to make any definitive statements. However, others have told me that neither are beneficial for the quality of meditation. If you indulge in these drinks, you will have to see what works for you.

To offer a full picture, I would also like to address psychedelic drugs which are used in the indigenous cultures of some countries to enable access to meditation and visions. I'm also unable to provide any information about my own experience in this area as I always found it more worthwhile to strive to expand the mind without any external aids. I do not encourage drug consumption; instead I recommend getting to know your mind so well that you feel enriched without the need for artificial stimulation.

Now you have obtained an overview on how wide aids for meditations might reach. It may be specific products or parts of your daily life. Now that you have got all the preparation done, you are ready to begin meditating.

Chapter 9

Top Tips for Beginners and Advanced Learners

Tips for beginners

Do you want to meditate, but don't know how? Many meditation beginners give up frustrated after a short period of time, as they believe that meditation has not worked for them. The reasons for this are often that they start with challenging passive meditation forms in sitting or have very high expectations, sometimes unrealistic, about what they're capable of.

But learning to meditate is like learning to walk. There are certain forms which are better suited to beginners. Active meditations facilitate entry to meditation, just as crawling helps young children to eventually walk.

Learning to walk requires continuity and perseverance. Meditation should also be seen as a long-term project, in which your ability slowly evolves over a period of years.

If you think that meditation has to work straightaway, you will have to reconsider your requirements. Just like learning a musical instrument, a foreign language or a new sport, meditation requires practice and training before you experience initial successes. Indeed, patience is one of the virtues which meditation teaches.

How can I learn to meditate?

Just like everything else, meditation first has to be learned. On a basic level, it is not particularly difficult. You will understand the process having done it only a couple of times.

But the real challenge—which the processes only serve as a vehicle for—is bringing peace to the mind and that is something which requires a lot of practice. However, as soon as meditation has become part of your daily routine, this provides the necessary continuity to ensure the required practice.

With a teacher

In my experience, it is difficult to find a meditation teacher who offers instruction in various forms. In other words, you have to decide on one meditation form in advance. You can find information on this in other parts of the book. This should make it easier to find the right teacher.

Most of the teaching on offer is in groups, but this is not necessarily our favorite option as Aspies. If there is a meditation center near you, ask for individual lessons so that you can reduce tiring interpersonal contact down to a minimum. Perhaps you can also find a teacher who is willing to come to your home.

Here are a few points to consider when selecting the right teacher: The teacher should of course have mastered the meditation form which you would like to learn. In addition, the teacher should be likeable, allowing you to relax in his or her presence. The good thing about learning to meditate is that you will not have to speak very much. However, you should feel comfortable enough to ask questions if you need to and let yourself go without any inhibitions.

Alone

Even if your entry to meditation would be easier with the teacher, it can of course also work alone. After all, when you learn meditation the primary focus is on the act itself. From that point of view, one hour a week with a teacher will not help you very much if you don't want to practice alone at home.

PREPARATIONS FOR LEARNING MEDITATION ALONE

Before you start meditating for the first time, you can optimize the conditions to suit your requirements. Therefore you should think about the following points in advance and ensure you have the necessary aids close by.

SELECTING A MEDITATION

The first important step is selecting your favored type of meditation. You can find plenty of information and inspiration on this in various parts of the book.

ADDITIONAL INSTRUCTIONS

Perhaps you would like to buy books, CDs or find more information online about the meditation form which you have selected.

However, please remember that all the rules which you read should be adjusted to suit your requirements. Meditation is not there to torture you. Note down the changes that you would like to make.

ADAPTING YOUR ROUTINE

Think about what time of day would be best for your meditation. Adjust your daily schedule to integrate a time window for meditation every day if possible. (See the section in Chapter 7 on "When should I meditate?")

SELECTING A LOCATION

Look for a location which caters to your requirements. Set up this location in such a way that you feel comfortable and you can meditate there safely. (See the section in Chapter 7 on "Where should I meditate?")

SELECTING CLOTHING

Select suitable clothing for your chosen meditation (see "And what should I wear?" in Chapter 7).

SELECTING MEDITATION AIDS

Read through Chapter 8 "Aids for Meditation" for possible aids which might help you and consider if any of these could offer a support. Actioning one or more of those tips may perhaps give yourself the best possible start in your meditation life.

Checklist for starting to meditate

Have I taken care of everything? Here's a list to copy and tick off:

- ☐ Comfortable clothing
- ☐ Informed the people around you that you do not want to be disturbed
- ☐ Telephone switched off
- ☐ Meditation space ready
- ☐ Instructions for meditation to hand
- ☐ Music ready
- ☐ Meditation book, paper and pen close by
- ☐ Alarm set to the desired time
- ☐ Other aids ready
- ☐ Glasses removed

Read the instructions through one more time before you begin.

If you want to, start by writing down your current state of mind and feelings in your meditation book.

Now you can get going!

It is quite simple: start meditating! That's the most important thing.

Just know that you cannot do anything wrong which can harm you. If you do not do something correctly, it does not have any damaging consequences. It is clear that if you try something new, it will not be easy right away.

Simply follow the instructions you have. If it gives you a certain amount of security, you can also check the instructions during meditation.

If you have thoughts of tasks you don't want to forget, then write them down on the paper nearby. The same applies if you have insights during meditation which you fear that you will forget—write these down in your meditation book.

After meditation

After ending your meditation, take some time to make some notes in your meditation book. How did you feel? How do you feel now? What thoughts did you experience? What thoughts are you having now? For more suggested questions, please read the section on meditation books in the previous chapter.

After the first couple of times that you meditate, check that all of the conditions were suitable for you. Were you distracted by anything (e.g. noise) around you? Was your clothing cozy and practical? Was your body comfortable? Did you perhaps miss a meditation aid?

If you find anything impacted your meditation, think about it and write down what you can change to improve the conditions for next time and then ensure you implement this. This is a good way of improving your meditation practice over time.

Perseverance

You can believe me when I say that I have often sat in meditation groups and "forced myself to meditate." I thought: "Man, when will it finally be over?!" I got incredibly bored because I didn't open myself up to the experience internally, even though I knew it would do me good in the long term. Indeed, the path also throws many obstacles in the way.

So how did I deal with situations like this? I used this simple but effective trick: if you "have to" meditate for another 30 minutes, imagine it is another three hours. Or 30 hours. Select an absurdly high number so that you simply give up inside. So high that you think "this will never end!" You resign yourself to it internally, to the unimaginably long time still to go. When you resign yourself to it, you break your inner wall of opposition. You give up and you are no longer defensive internally. You are no longer against something, but instead open to it. You are resigned but open. This gives you the space for a new experience.

The alternative would be to stop the meditation annoyed and frustrated. A poor choice. By not stopping, you are at least giving yourself the chance to do a meditation which enriches you. If you give up, you have not achieved anything for yourself. Give yourself a chance—you are worth it!

Am I doing it right?

This is a question which haunts beginners. Being caught with doubts is understandable when you learn something new. Just because you have doubts doesn't mean that you are doing it wrong. It only means that you are serious about it and that you are making an effort to do it correctly.

I would first like to calm your doubts. If you follow the tips from my book as best you can, then the obvious answer is: yes, you are doing it right!

It is normal for it to work better on some days than others. Just continue doing it every day and it will get better.

Perhaps this won't assure everyone. Here are a few more tips for the more stubborn of you: if you continue to wonder whether you are "doing it right," I suggest talking to someone who is experienced in meditation. That might be a friend or acquaintance who practices on a regular basis. If you don't have someone like this around you or if this doesn't help you, it is perhaps a good idea to ask someone who is involved with meditation on a professional level. This might be a meditation teacher near you. You can read about how to find the right person at the start of this chapter. Perhaps you can even find someone like me who knows about Asperger's and can address your individual needs.

When it comes to meditation, it is often simpler to work with someone near you, but it is also possible over long distances. I support clients abroad via email and Skype, for instance.

Be responsible, take care of yourself and look for support. If you have consciously decided to pursue meditation, you will certainly find someone who can help you if you have any doubts. Remind yourself of the virtues of persistence, patience and hope.

When your mind is too loud

This eternal topic affects everyone who meditates, whether beginner or advanced learner.

It is the reason that I most commonly hear when I ask clients why they don't meditate (any more).

Paradoxically, it is the same reason that I hear most often when I ask clients why they wanted to meditate in the first place.

"It is too loud in my mind, that's why I want to meditate, but I can't meditate because it is too loud in my mind." A vicious circle. But if you give up meditation because of this, you've not gained anything: it is still loud in your mind. It is difficult but in the long term more satisfying to break this vicious circle and enhance your quality of life. However, it wouldn't be called a vicious circle if it wasn't viciously difficult to break! Nevertheless, I can promise you that it is worth your while.

When it comes to the Aspie mind, which takes on board so many of the stimuli from everyday life, it is really worthwhile for your personal well-being to make time to process these stimuli. To be still, to find peace, to let your thoughts go and realize you do not have to give them your consideration.

The Americans call it a "monkey mind" if your head doesn't allow you to relax. When one thought leads to the next, from one stimulus to the next. If I may say so, this is normal during meditation. It's no different for NTs. As I said, you shouldn't be disheartened because that is what meditation is all about—quieting the mind.

I have plenty of personal experience of this monkey mind. For years, my mind was always jumping from one thing to the next and it still does today before I start meditation following an action-packed day. I needed many years of continuous meditation practice to master the monkey on my mind. Vince Lombardi once said: "It's not whether you get knocked down; it's whether you get up" (see Lombardi 2010). Perseverance and patience are key to achieving lasting change. Nowadays I'm able to succeed in this, so I concentrate on taking care of the peace in my mind, which represents the source of strength in my life.

Here are some tried and tested tips for combating the monkey mind.

Occupy yourself

Occupying yourself forms the basis of all these tips. In simple terms: allow your mind to take part in the meditation. Give it something to do during meditation. Occupy it so it doesn't occupy you (for more on this, please read "Meditation and mind" in Chapter 3).

This is generally easier in an active meditation, which is why I advise beginners to start with this form of meditation.

Posture and face

Direct your concentration to your body's posture. Where is your body bending? Where is it stretching? How is your weight distributed? Which body parts are touching each other? You can also slightly shift your weight from side to side in order to follow the change with your mind.

You can also direct your concentration to your face, or the expression you have. Which muscles are tensed and which are relaxed?

Please note that there is no correct or incorrect posture. It is quite possible that you can make your posture even more comfortable or relax certain muscles even more. But don't judge yourself harshly, simply notice it and respond to it.

Body

Allow yourself to explore your body with your thoughts and invite your mind to accompany you. Begin with your right foot and feel what it feels. Feel which parts of your foot are touching the floor, feel the pressure against it, feel the consistency of the material and anything else which you notice. Describe it in your mind. For instance: "My right foot is touching the upper side of the pillow. I can feel my sock against the sole of my foot. I can feel my little toe touching the toe next to it. I can feel pressure on the top of my foot but the foot is still relaxed."

You will notice—perhaps even be amazed—that your body consists of all these individual parts which can be observed.

Movements

If you've decided to do an active meditation, then your body is in movement. This at least gives your body something to occupy it and you can also integrate your mind into this.

Focus your concentration on to following this movement. Your mind can describe what your arms, legs, feet, head and neck are doing at that moment. In concrete terms, you are allowing your mind to describe yourself and what you're doing at that moment. For instance: "I am lifting my arm. I am exhaling. My weight is shifting forwards." I'm sure that this won't get boring and it also leaves you with no time for a monkey mind. This helps your body and mind to form a union, which is an excellent prerequisite for deep meditation.

Rocking

I know that many Aspies like rocking as it often helps to calm them down. If that is also the case for you, then allow yourself to rock and focus your concentration on this subtle movement. Feel how it shifts the weight. Feel the various parts of the body carrying this weight. You can tune the rhythm of your rocking into the rhythm of your breathing or count your rocking movements as described in this chapter. If you have read in meditation instructions that you have to sit still, then forget that. You decide how you meditate and if rocking helps you, then do it!

Relaxation

Mental relaxation comes through physical relaxation. Most people find it easier to relax their body on command than they do their mind—otherwise meditation wouldn't be so difficult.

If the body is relaxed, then the mind finds it easier to follow these feelings. Therefore, the first step is to relax the body.

We often don't even realize how tense we are physically as we get used to a certain amount of muscular tension over time and eventually see this as the normal state of affairs.

One way to achieve physical relaxation is the method of progressive muscle relaxation. In progressive muscle relaxation, individual parts of the body are first consciously tensed, with this tension lasting for a few seconds in order to then consciously relax. This method is very easy to learn. If you are interested, you will find plenty of books, CDs, courses and websites with more information on this topic.

One area which is often forgotten when relaxing is the face. Therefore I would like to address that here. To relax your face follow these simple steps:

- Relax your eyes, relax your vision, release your focus and allow everything to be blurred.

- Or close your eyes and imagine you are looking at something in the far distance.

- Relax your forehead.

- Relax your jaw, allowing your upper and lower jaw to separate. Allow your lower jaw to drop slightly, leaving your mouth open a touch.

- Relax your tongue. Allow it to move away from your gums and lie relaxed in your mouth.

- Breathe in.

- And then breathe out slowly.
- Breathe so deeply that it fills your entire belly.
- And then let it out.

Counting

Count your breaths, from 1 to 10 or from 10 to 1. When you reach the last number, start again. If your thoughts interrupt the counting, simply begin again from the start. When I first began meditating, I needed a very long time until I could reach 10. But that's okay. Meditation is not a counting competition. The counting simply serves to occupy the mind. Your breathing is the basis for your body. Both serve to nourish your soul.

Meditation beads

You can also use meditation beads to occupy your mind. Count the beads with your fingers and your mind to your own inner rhythm or the pace of your breathing (see "Aids for Meditation" in previous chapter).

Breathing

Focus on your breathing. Observe how you breathe in… And breathe out… And then there is a natural small pause. And then you breathe in again… And breathe out.

You can commentate on this natural flow in your head with the words "breathe in," "breathe out" and "pause."

Mantras

If you decided to do a mantra meditation, then the mantra is a good starting point which you can focus your concentration on. Here it is only natural for your thoughts to wander somewhat, but the mantra always gives you the opportunity to refocus your mind and constantly occupy it.

The "Extras" approach

As I said at the start of the book, the promise of meditation and one of the main reasons which moves people to start meditating is to quiet thoughts and balance the mind.

If you are now meditating but your thoughts are not quieting despite expectation and hope, you can quickly get caught up in thoughts such as: "My mind has to be quiet! I'm not allowed to think of anything!" It is no wonder that it doesn't work in this case, just as the statement "Don't think of pink elephants" will inevitably lead to thoughts of pink elephants.

The mental approach should be that you allow your head to be loud. Thoughts may come and go as they please and they are allowed to be there. But you don't have to pay attention to them. Allow them to speak. They remain extras in the background of a film in which you are playing a leading role. And while the thoughts speak, you continue to meditate.

Passing clouds

If you notice that thoughts are emerging, simply let them wash over you. There is an image which I found difficult to implement to start with, but which over the years has helped create a peaceful atmosphere in situations where the monkey mind is in full flow:

> Imagine you are a mountain lake and your thoughts move over you like clouds in the sky, far above you and in peace. It is okay that they are there, but you don't have to give them any attention. They reflect themselves in you. You throw their reflection back towards them and the wind blows them away.

Generally, this technique is more suitable for advanced learners because it works easiest when you have already developed a certain feel for your thoughts. It can also quite easily lead to you actually following the monkey mind thoughts by accident.

Stubborn apes?

In all probability, the monkey mind will make itself felt once again despite your best efforts. But that doesn't matter. If you notice that this is the case, refocus again and simply continue. You will see that over the course of a long period of time things will improve. Have some patience with yourself and don't be annoyed if your thoughts wander now and again. That's perfectly normal and does not have any negative consequences. Simply continue to meditate.

You might protest against all these tricks for combating the monkey mind: "Yes, my mind might not be thinking about the shopping list any more but instead it's thinking about my body or the number of breaths I'm taking. But it continues to speak loud and clear!" That may be true. But it is now speaking more sense. And I'll tell you why: no matter which of these tips you choose to use, your mind is always in the here and now. It counts the breath you are currently taking. It describes how your foot is currently positioned. Your mind is therefore not in the past ("I really didn't feel comfortable during my meeting with Ms. F. this morning") and not in the future ("after meditating I have to go and buy some bread"), but in the present. And that is what meditation is all about.

Tips for advanced learners

If you've made the decision to get into close contact with yourself, meditation becomes a process which accompanies you through your life, making it a lifelong learning experience. You can make meditation into a life-changing, enriching method for more balance, meaning and personal fulfillment in your life.

If you are committed to practicing meditation over a long period of time, you will gradually be able to observe how the pure effect of relaxation is enriched through personal insight.

In this phase, you may still have questions or long for general discussion about meditation. This was certainly the case in my experience and in my work with other advanced learners.

The topics addressed by advanced learners are wide ranging. For instance, some say that they used meditation primarily for relaxation up to a point and now a new curiosity has emerged about what remains to be discovered. Others don't have the confidence to restart their regular meditation practice after a long break and need some help getting started again. Or perhaps meditation has become too monotone and they would like to try out a new form of meditation. New forms of meditation offer new challenges—both physical and mental—enabling new thought patterns and new experiences.

Some clients also described the feeling of stagnation, which can stem from personal attitude, expectations or technique. Others have experienced something in meditation which they would like to discuss professionally. In my practice, I reflect and meditate with them in an effort to identify a way of opening new paths.

At this point in the book, I would like to address a few of these points and provide some answers to these individual issues as best I can.

Using meditation for everyday life

If you have had a positive meditation experience, you will probably want to maintain this feeling throughout your everyday life. Here's a tip about succeeding in doing this:

> After you have the experience, attempt to formulate and write down a description of it as tangibly as possible. Use insights from all your senses. If the feeling was a color, which would it be? How big? What material? What are the characteristics of its surface? What consistency? What smell? What sound would it make?

This perhaps sounds strange at first but these comparisons can help you recall feelings at a later date. To practice this, first select a peaceful situation, such as when you are in bed at night. Then remind yourself of your description of the feeling, with all the attributes which you noted down. Then attempt to feel what you felt once again. If you're able to recall this in peaceful and stress-free situations, you can also practice doing the same in stressful situations. In this way you equip yourself with the ability to calm down despite stress.

Increasing training

Has meditation been working well up to now? You are increasingly succeeding in putting yourself in a peaceful state after a short time in every meditation, turning off internally and strengthening yourself mentally? Are you looking for a new challenge? Then try this:

> In order to train the process of sinking into meditation and to intensify it, it is helpful to increase the amount of outside stimuli—in other words, distractions. Consciously put yourself in

situations with a lot of distractions. For example, turn the radio or TV on while meditating.

Or find distracting locations and attempt to meditate there. This could be a park bench, a bus station, the subway or a walking meditation in the supermarket. You might even find that the stress level there is already lower than it was previously.

Meditating on something

To meditate on something, whether it be a question, a decision, a wish or anything else is an activity for advanced learners.

Meditating on something is a powerful tool for answering life's questions. It allows you to find answers which don't just come from your logical brain, but which stem from your feelings and are supported by all levels of consciousness. These are answers which are not possible in everyday life, and perhaps not accessible. Advanced meditation opens your consciousness and enables new perspectives, allowing you to shed new light on old topics.

Why is it so difficult to meditate on something? Well, as you've seen up to now, meditation is about letting your thoughts go, allowing them to pass over you and not giving them any attention. In conventional meditation, life questions are intentionally left alone and solutions are allowed to develop during meditation without forcing them.

At first glance, meditating on a question in fact seems to contradict this intention to be thought-free. After all, the meditation time shouldn't be used to think about a question—that would certainly be difficult without any thoughts! However, if you would like to meditate on something, the question is the focus of your attention. That's what makes this so challenging—thinking about something without thinking about it.

The first step is therefore to learn to not think about anything, as described in the book so far.

I would now like to describe how you take the next step to meditating on something. As it is very difficult to find the right words for this personal inner process, my language might be a little more imprecise here and it may require a little feeling, imagination and experience on your part to understand my points.

First, it is important to be aware of the exact question you are dealing with. Crystallize in your mind the topic which you would like to address. Attempt to reduce it down to one sentence, so that you define the essence.

To start your meditation, focus your mind on the topic. Fill your intellect and brain with it. Then subsequently expand it to include your feelings. Feel the question, be aware of what impact it has on you emotionally. Let it float in your heart. Fill your whole being with this question on every level.

Here is the trick: now let the thought go. Let it drift out of your mind. Release the thought from your emotions. Allow it to float away from your heart. Give yourself over to meditation again as usual.

Meanwhile, the echo of the question will continue to sound in the back of your consciousness. When you have found peace in the meditation, cautiously draw on this echo—perceive it, feel it, open it with your consciousness, sense it from all sides, bask in its resonance, illuminate it from your place of meditation. Feel its various facets and variations, sense solutions, ways and connections—and then let them go again.

Using this technique, an answer will be formed in your consciousness over time—in one meditation session or several. It may come as a thought, a feeling, a soft insight or a brainwave—the answer could take many forms.

Real reality?

Under this heading, I'd like to describe a couple of thought models which could help you to see your environment, and therefore yourself, from a different perspective.

Taking a new perspective requires the willingness to question what you have believed up to this point. I think that we as Aspies are quite well versed in this procedure as we have to question a lot of things in our perception over and over again in order to adjust to the general perception of society. This difference between our individual perception and that of other people is an everyday part of our lives and consciousness.

Advanced meditation allows you to look at things from a new perspective, to question your reality up to now and to meditate more deeply, paving the way for profound personal experience.

The ancient Greek philosopher Plato already created a hypothetical scenario, known as *The Allegory of the Cave* (to be found in book VII of his work *The Republic*), with which he shows the individual perspective of reality. Let me give you a short, personal summary of it, where I emphasize the perspective that supports my intention to talk about reality: Plato speaks of people, chained to a wall in a cave, who just see shadows of the people living outside of the cave—and the prisoners take that for reality, as that is all they know. One day some of them escape, discover the world outside and realize that they don't want to spend the rest of their lives in the cave. Nevertheless they go back into the cave to tell their people about the outside world. But they don't believe them, laugh at them and assure them that they will never ever leave their cave, their world (summarized from Allen 2008).

Plato opens questions that invite us to think about what we take for reality. Do we call our world reality just because we see it every day? Is that all there is? Is what other people see less real? Are we open-minded to change this approach when someone presents us with a new perspective on it?

A modern interpretation of this scenario would involve being chained in a cinema in front of a screen. Or—even more futuristic—living in a Holodeck, like those featured in *Star Trek*. Or in the Matrix, as in the film of the same name.

No matter which version of the story appeals to you most, the thinking behind it is the same: is the world really as it seems to you? Is your reality really what you think it is? If so, how does it look for other people? Or is there more to it? If so, what? And who?

I don't want to attempt to answer these questions or quote famous philosophers' take on them. I don't want to spoil your fun! Only your answer counts. Your experience. Your meditation.

The white wall

In the film *The Matrix* (1999), there is a white place called "the construct," which Neo and Morpheus visit at the start of Neo's training. It is a purely white place—a white room with invisible walls, floor and ceiling. A place seemingly without any dimensions. In this room, Morpheus' crew can load the content which is needed at specific times.

The white wall from Zazen tradition can have a similar effect. In Zazen, people meditate with eyes open in front of a white wall. The wall is the only thing they see.

Give this short thought experiment a try:

> Sit in front of a white wall. The white wall sits in front of you. The wall is everything you are. Everything you have ever been and will ever be is this white wall. All your wishes, dreams, desires, fears and worries are this white wall. The white wall is your question for life as well as the answer to the

question. Be the wall. And the wall becomes you. Who is meditating, you or the wall? Both?

Recommended films
The films *The Matrix* (1999), *The Truman Show* (1998), *The Sixth Sense* (1999), *Being John Malkovich* (1999), *Inception* (2012) and *The Adjustment Bureau* (2011) are all excellent starting points for rethinking your own reality. How do you consider your reality? Is it as real as you think? How can you be sure? Because you can see it? Because you can touch it? Because you can feel it? Because you want it to exist? Try watching these films and continue to meditate.

Final thoughts
I'm drawing my book to a conclusion now in the knowledge of having said everything that was necessary.

I hope that I was able to inspire you and that you now have the courage to start meditating. I would be delighted if my book has helped you to discover meditation for yourself.

Even if it hasn't, I would be equally as delighted if my book has given you something else which may enable you to lead a more autonomous Aspie life with a higher quality of living from now on. Perhaps you would like to share your successes with me? I am always thrilled to hear from readers.

Following my diagnosis and extensive sessions with clients, I am sometimes completely amazed by how much I've learned over the years. I found it very easy to write this book. I already had all the knowledge inside me, it just had to come out and be bent into shape. Now you hold this knowledge in your hands.

The book may be over, but you have a long journey in front of you. Enjoy a relaxing voyage of discovery. I hope you find a gateway to your inner home and your inner source of peace, balance and insight.

Now there's nothing more to say other than: have fun meditating! Put the book away and let's go!

About the Author

Ulrike Domenika Bolls, born in 1972, studied design and then began supporting people in crisis situations parallel to her main career. She dedicated a lot of time to self-discovery in therapies and seminars in Germany and the United States, before she began working on a self-employed basis with people in transformation processes in 2000.

She started learning meditation aged 20 and received the positive diagnosis of Asperger Syndrome in her adult years. This explains her dedication to this meditation technique, which has played a major role in her life up to now.

Nowadays she offers coaching for gifted and highly sensitive people both with and without Asperger Syndrome under the name Highmat®, as well as introductory courses, support and training in meditation.

She has been married since 1998 and she lives with her husband in Munich, Germany.

You can get more details and contact information at www. gifted-coaching.com

This is the author's fifth published book, but her first in English. Her previous four books appeared in German and also focused on meditation and self-discovery.

Meditation for Aspies was translated from German into English by Rowan Sewell. Rowan Sewell is a freelance translator from the Peak District in Great Britain. He currently lives with his partner in Passau, Germany.

References

The Adjustment Bureau (2011) Director: George Nolfi. Writers: George Nolfi (screenplay), Philip K. Dick (short story "Adjustment Team"). Actors: Matt Damon, Emily Blunt. Production Companies: Universal Pictures, Media Rights Capital, Gambit Pictures.

Aeoliah (1998) Angel Love. Audio CD. Label: Oreade.

Allen, R. (trans.) (2008) *Plato: The Republic* (2nd edition). New Haven, CT: Yale University Press.

Being John Malkovich (1999) Director: Spike Jonze. Writer: Charlie Kaufman. Actors: John Cusack, Cameron Diaz, John Malkovich. Production Companies: Gramercy Pictures (I), Propaganda Films, Single Cell Pictures.

A Brief History of Time (1991) Director: Errol Morris. Writer: Stephen Hawking (book). Starring Stephen Hawking, Isobel Hawking. Production Companies: Amblin Entertainment, Anglia Television, Channel Four Films.

Inception (2012) Director: Christopher Nolan. Writer: Christopher Nolan. Actors: Leonardo DiCaprio, Joseph Gordon-Levitt. Production Companies: Warner Bros. Pictures, Legendary Pictures, Syncopy.

Lombardi, V. (2010) *Famous Quotes by Vincent Lombardi*. Available at www.vincelombardi.com/quotes.html, accessed on December 3, 2012.

MacInnes, E. and Habito, R. L. F. (2007) *The Flowing Bridge: Guidance on Beginning Zen Koans*. Somerville, MA: Wisdom Publications.

The Matrix (1999) Director: The Wachowski Brothers. Actors: Keanu Reeves, Laurence Fishburne. Studio: Warner Home Video. DVD release date: May 15, 2007.

Murphy, M. and Donovan, S. (1997) *The Physical and Psychological Effects of Meditation*. Petaluma, CA: Institute of Noetic Sciences.

Schlütter, M. (2008) *How Zen Became Zen: The Dispute over Enlightenment and the Formation of Chan Buddhism in Song-Dynasty China.* Honolulu: University of Hawai'i Press.

The Sixth Sense (1999) Director: M. Night Shyamalan. Writer: M. Night Shyamalan. Actors: Bruce Willis, Haley Joel Osment, Production Companies: Barry Mendel Productions, Hollywood Pictures, Kennedy/ Marshall Company.

Thich Nhat Hanh (1998) "Public Lecture." Retreat led by Thich Nhat Hanh, November 9, 1998, Zirkus-Krone-Bau, Munich, Germany.

The Truman Show (1998) Director: Peter Weir. Actors: Jim Carrey, Ed Harris. Producers: Adam Schroeder, Andrew Niccol, Edward S. Feldman, Lynn Pleshette, Richard Luke Rothschild. Studio: Paramount.

Yamada, K. (2004) *The Gateless Gate: The Classic Book of Zen Koans.* Foreword by Ruben L. F. Habito. Somerville, MA: Wisdom Publications.

Useful Resources

Breema

Breema Center website: www.breema.com

Schreiber, J. (1998) *Breema*. Berkeley, CA: North Atlantic Books.

Schreiber, J. (2007) *Breema and the Nine Principles of Harmony* (1st edition). Oakland, CA: Breema Center Publishing.

Schreiber, J. and Berezonsky, D. (2001) *Self-Breema: Exercises for Harmonious Life*. Oakland, CA: California Health Publications.

Relaxation methods

McManus, C. (2003) *Progressive Relaxation and Autogenic Training*. Audio CD. Carolyn McManus.

Salcedo, B. (2007) *Progressive Muscle Relaxation: 20 Minutes to Total Relaxation*. Audio CD. Beth Salcedo, MD.

Guided imagery

Bryant, C. and Weaver, C. (2003) *Night Time Moods: Guided Imagery for Children*. Bloomington. IN: 1st Book Library.

Joseph, L. (2008) *Emotional Renewal Guided Imagery for Caregivers: Looking After Yourself While Helping a Loved One*. Audio CD (1st edition). Release date: April 3, 2008. Discovery Dynamics, Inc.

Lusk, J. T. (1992–93) *30 Scripts for Relaxation, Imagery and Inner Healing* (vol. 1, 1992; vol. 2, 1993). Duluth, MN: Whole Person Associates.

Nourishing TV

The Aquarium DVD (2009) Fullscreen edition of fish aquarium.

Earth from Above (2011) Starring Yann Arthus-Bertrand. DVD release date: April 19, 2011.

Fireplace DVD: Real Wood Burning Fire (2008) Anamorphic—fullscreen edition of fireplace.

Planet Earth: The Complete BBC Series (2007) Starring David Attenborough. DVD release date: April 24, 2007. BBC Worldwide.

Nourishing exercise

Wildman, F. (2006) *Feldenkrais: The Busy Person's Guide to Easier Movement.* Berkeley, CA: The Intelligent Body Press.

Dynamic meditation

Deuter and Osho (2000) *OSHO Dynamic Meditation.* Audio CD. Release date: June 26, 2000. New Earth Records.

Koan meditation

Loori, J. D. and Kirchner, T. (2005) *Sitting with Koans: Essential Writings on the Zen Practice of Koan Study.* Somerville, MA: Wisdom Publications.

MacInnes, E. and Habito, R. L. F. (2007) *The Flowing Bridge: Guidance on Beginning Zen Koans.* Somerville, MA: Wisdom Publications.

Mumon (2008) *The Gateless Gate: A Collection of Zen Koan.* St Petersburg, FL: Red and Black Publishers.

Painting mandalas

Gauding, M. (2006) *World Mandalas: 100 New Designs for Coloring and Meditation.* London: Godsfield.

Mandali, M. (1998) *Everyone's Mandala Coloring Book* (vol. 1). [Vol. 2 in 2001.] Helena, MT: Mandali Publishing.

Sundberg, J. and Ahlquist, M. (2006) *Journey In: A Meditative Coloring Journal* (2nd edition). Alexandria, MN: Journey-In.

Sitting meditation

Meditation aids such as cushions and benches.

Sitting aids and supplies in general

DharmaCrafts: www.dharmacrafts.com

Four Gates: www.fourgates.com

MeditationBench.com: www.meditationbench.com

Samadhi Cushions: www.samadhicushions.com

Sitting aids

Back Jack Europe: www.backjack-europe.com

Benchbow: www.benchbow.com/lang1

B.J. Industries: www.backjackusa.com

Sitting aids for traveling

Sunburst Meditation Cushion: www.sunburstmeditationcushion.co.uk

Wisdom Travelers: www.wisdomtravelers.com

Music
Deuter

Deuter and Osho. *OSHO Dynamic Meditation* (2000) Audio CD. Original release date: June 26, 2000. New Earth Records.

Deuter and Osho. *OSHO Nadabrahma Meditation* (1992) Audio CD. Original release date: January 1, 1992. New Earth Records.

Mantras

Premal, Deva (1998) *The Essence.* Audio CD. Original release date: June 1, 1998. White Swan.

Premal, Deva (2010) *Mantras for Precarious Times.* Audio CD. Original release date: February 2, 2010. White Swan.

Tuning forks

Biosonics: www.biosonics.com/Tuning-Forks

Meditation teachers

The purpose of this book is to help you to start meditating on your own. You have got all you need so you can start any time you want.

My editor asked me to include specific information on how to find out about meditation teachers and classes. I find it hard to recommend general addresses, as the world is so big, the range of meditation forms is equally big and the personal needs, dislikes and likes are so different. I couldn't find a webpage that offers an intelligent search mask where you enter your desired form of meditation, your location and on the press of a button a teacher's address pops out.

Hence my best suggestion is—as it is the spirit of my book to encourage you to take responsibility for your life—when you feel in need of a teacher, to start your own internet research, containing your location and desired meditation to find appropriate teachers and classes.

Meditation forms

There is such a wide range of meditation forms that it can become quite confusing. This is why I picked out a couple of techniques that cover a wide range of different approaches. If you want to find more methods, help yourself on the internet—for example, on these pages that offer a short introduction in different meditation techniques:

ABC of Meditation: www.abc-of-meditation.com/meditation-techniques

ABC of Yoga: www.abc-of-yoga.com/meditation/techniques.asp

About.com Stress Management: stress.about.com/od/lowstresslifestyle/a/meditation.htm

Project-Meditation: www.project-meditation.org/meditation_techniques.html

Index